PENGUIN  CLASSICS

THE MIS-EDUCATION OF THE NEGRO

CARTER GODWIN WOODSON (1875–1950) was the child and student of formerly enslaved people. He was born in Buckingham County, Virginia, and graduated from West Virginia's Frederick Douglass High School in 1896. Woodson earned degrees from Berea College and the University of Chicago, before becoming the second African American to receive a PhD from Harvard in 1912, after W. E. B. Du Bois. Woodson began his career as a schoolteacher in the 1890s, remaining in this profession until 1919. He worked in the public schools of West Virginia, the Philippines, and Washington, DC, where he taught at the famous Paul Laurence Dunbar High School. Woodson founded the Association for the Study of Negro Life and History in 1915, *The Journal of Negro History* in 1916, and Negro History Week in 1926, which is now celebrated as Black History Month.

JARVIS R. GIVENS is an assistant professor at the Harvard Graduate School of Education and a faculty affiliate in the department of African and African American Studies at Harvard University. Givens earned his PhD in African American Studies from the University of California, Berkeley, and he is the author of *Fugitive Pedagogy: Carter G. Woodson and the Art of Black Teaching*, which won the 2022 Association for the Study of African American Life and History Book Prize and the 2022 Outstanding Book Award from the American Educational Research Association.

HENRY LOUIS GATES, JR., is the Alphonse Fletcher University Professor and founding director of the Hutchins Center for African and African American Research at Harvard University. He is editor in chief of the Oxford African American Studies Center and TheRoot.com, and creator of the highly praised PBS documentary *The African Americans: Many Rivers to Cross*. He is the general editor for a Penguin Classics series of African American works.

CARTER G. WOODSON

The Mis-education
of the Negro

Introduction by
JARVIS R. GIVENS

General Editor:
HENRY LOUIS GATES, JR.

PENGUIN BOOKS

PENGUIN BOOKS
An imprint of Penguin Random House LLC
penguinrandomhouse.com

This Penguin Classics edition reprints Carter G. Woodson's original
1933 edition and includes the standardization of terms.

LIBRARY OF CONGRESS CATALOGING-IN-PUBLICATION DATA
Names: Woodson, Carter Godwin, 1875–1950, author. |
Gates, Henry Louis, Jr., editor.
Title: The mis-education of the Negro / Carter G. Woodson ; introduction by
Jarvis R. Givens ; general editor, Henry Louis Gates, Jr..
Other titles: Miseducation of the Negro
Description: New York : Penguin Books, 2023. | Series: Penguin classics |
Originally published: Washington, D.C. : Associated Publishers, c1933. |
Includes bibliographical references and index.
Identifiers: LCCN 2022026945 (print) | LCCN 2022026946 (ebook) |
ISBN 9780143137467 (paperback) | ISBN 9780593511534 (ebook)
Subjects: LCSH: African Americans—Education. |
Discrimination in education—United States. | African Americans—
Social conditions—To 1964. | African Americans—Employment.
Classification: LCC LC2717.W6 2023 (print) | LCC LC2717 (ebook) |
DDC 371.829/96073—dc23/eng/20220804
LC record available at https://lccn.loc.gov/2022026945
LC ebook record available at https://lccn.loc.gov/2022026946

Printed in the United States of America
1st Printing

Set in Sabon LT Pro

Contents

THE MIS-EDUCATION OF THE NEGRO

What Is an
African American Classic?

I have long nurtured a deep and abiding affection for the Penguin Classics, at least since I was an undergraduate at Yale. I used to imagine that my attraction for these books—grouped together, as a set, in some independent bookstores when I was a student, and perhaps even in some today—stemmed from the fact that my first-grade classmates, for some reason that I can't recall, were required to dress as penguins in our annual all-school pageant, and perform a collective side-to-side motion that our misguided teacher thought she could choreograph into something meant to pass for a "dance." Piedmont, West Virginia, in 1956, was a very long way from Penguin Nation, wherever that was supposed to be! But penguins we were determined to be, and we did our level best to avoid wounding each other with our orange-colored cardboard beaks while stomping out of rhythm in our matching orange, veined webbed feet. The whole scene was madness, one never to be repeated at the Davis Free School. But I never stopped loving penguins. And I have never stopped loving the very audacity of the idea of the Penguin Classics, an affordable, accessible library of the most important and compelling texts in the history of civilization, their black-and-white spines and covers and uniform type giving each text a comfortable, familiar feel, as if we have encountered it, or its cousins, before. I think of the Penguin Classics as the very best and most compelling in human thought, an Alexandrian library in paperback, enclosed in black and white.

I still gravitate to the Penguin Classics when killing time in an airport bookstore, deferring the slow torture of the security lines. Sometimes I even purchase two or three, fantasizing that I can speed-read one of the shorter titles, then make a dent in the longer one, vainly attempting to fill the holes in the liberal arts education that our degrees suggest we have, over the course of a plane ride! Mark Twain once quipped that a classic is "something that everybody wants to have read and nobody wants to read," and perhaps that applies to my airport purchasing habits. For my generation, these titles in the Penguin Classics form the canon—the canon of the texts that a truly well-educated person should have read, and read carefully and closely, at least once. For years I rued the absence of texts by black authors in this series, and longed to be able to make even a small contribution to the diversification of this astonishingly universal list. I watched with great pleasure as titles by African American and African authors began to appear, some two dozen over the past several years. So when Elda Rotor approached me about editing a series of African American classics and collections for Penguin's Portable Series, I eagerly accepted.

Thinking about the titles appropriate for inclusion in these series led me, inevitably, to think about what, for me, constitutes a "classic." And thinking about this led me, in turn, to the wealth of reflections on what defines a work of literature or philosophy somehow speaking to the human condition beyond time and place, a work somehow endlessly compelling, generation upon generation, a work whose author we don't have to look like to identify with, to feel at one with, as we find ourselves transported through the magic of a textual time machine; a work that refracts the image of ourselves that we project onto it, regardless of our ethnicity, our gender, our time, our place. This is what centuries of scholars and writers have meant when they use the word *classic*, and—despite all that we know about the complex intersubjectivity of the production of meaning in the wondrous exchange between a reader and a text—it remains true that classic texts, even in the most conventional, conservative sense of the word *classic*, do exist, and these books will continue to be read long after the generation the text reflects and defines, the generation of readers contemporary with the text's author, is dead and gone. Classic texts speak from their authors' graves, in their names, in their voices. As Italo Calvino once remarked, "A classic is a book that has never finished saying what it has to say."

Faulkner put this idea in an interesting way: "The aim of every artist is to arrest motion, which is life, by artificial means, and hold it fixed so that a hundred years later, when a stranger looks at it, it moves again since it is life." That, I am certain, must be the desire of every writer. But what about the reader? What makes a book a classic to a reader? Here, perhaps, Hemingway said it best: "All good books are alike in that they are truer than if they had really happened and after you are finished reading one you will feel that all that happened to you, and afterward it belongs to you, the good and the bad, the ecstasy, the remorse and sorrow, the people and the places and how the weather was."

I have been reading black literature since I was fifteen, yanked into the dark discursive universe by an Episcopal priest at a church camp near my home in West Virginia in August 1965, during the terrifying days of the Watts Riots in Los Angeles. Eventually, by fits and starts, studying the literature written by black authors became my avocation; ultimately, it has become my vocation. And, in my own way, I have tried to be an evangelist for it, to a readership larger than my own people, people who, as it were, look like these texts. Here, I am reminded of something W. S. Merwin said about the books he most loved: "Perhaps a classic is a work that one imagines should be common knowledge, but more and more often isn't." I would say, of African and African American literature, that perhaps classic works by black writers are works that one imagines should be common knowledge among the broadest possible readership but that less and less are, as the teaching of reading to understand how words can create the worlds into which books can transport us yields to classroom instruction geared toward passing a state-authorized standardized exam. All literary texts suffer from this wrongheaded approach to teaching, mind you; but it especially affects texts by people of color, and texts by women—texts still struggling, despite enormous gains over the last twenty years, to gain a solid foothold in anthologies and syllabi. For every anthology, every syllabus, every publishing series such as the Penguin Classics constitutes a distinct "canon," an implicit definition of all that is essential for a truly educated person to read.

James Baldwin, who has pride of place in my personal canon of African American authors since it was one of his books that that Episcopal priest gave me to read in that dreadful summer of 1965, argued that "the responsibility of a writer is to excavate the experience of the people who produced him." But surely Baldwin would have agreed with E. M. Forster that the books that we remember, the books that have truly influenced us, are those that "have gone a little further down our particular path than we have yet ourselves." Excavating the known is a worthy goal of the writer as cultural archeologist; yet, at the same time, so is unveiling the unknown, the unarticulated yet shared experience of the colorless things that make us human: "something we have always known (or thought we knew)," as Calvino puts it, "but without knowing that this author said it first." We might think of the difference between Forster and Baldwin, on the one hand, and Calvino, on the other, as the difference between an author representing what has happened (Forster, Baldwin) in the history of a people whose stories, whose very history itself, has long been suppressed, and what could have happened (Calvino) in the atemporal realm of art. This is an important distinction when thinking about the nature of an African American classic—rather, when thinking about the nature of the texts that constitute the African American literary tradition or, for that matter, the texts in any under-read tradition.

One of James Baldwin's most memorable essays, a subtle meditation on sexual preference, race, and gender, is entitled "Here Be Dragons." So much of traditional African American literature, even fiction and poetry—ostensibly at least once removed from direct statement—was meant to deal a fatal blow to the dragon of racism. For black writers since the eighteenth-century beginnings of the tradition, literature has been one more weapon—a very important weapon, mind you, but still one weapon among many—in the arsenal black people have drawn upon to fight against antiblack racism and for their equal rights before the law. Ted Joans, the black surrealist poet, called this sort of literature from the sixties' Black Arts Movement "hand grenade poems." Of what possible use are the niceties of figuration when one must slay a dragon? I can hear you say, give me the blunt weapon anytime! Problem is, it is more difficult than some writers seem to think to slay a dragon with a poem or a novel. Social problems persist; literature too tied to addressing those social problems tends to enter the historical archives, leaving the realm of the literary. Let me state bluntly what should be obvious: Writers are read for how they write, not what they write about.

Frederick Douglass—for this generation of readers one of the most widely read writers—reflected on this matter even in the midst of one of his most fiery speeches addressing the ironies of the sons and daughters of slaves celebrating the Fourth of July while slavery continued unabated. In his now-classic essay "What to the Slave Is the Fourth of July?" (1852), Douglass argued that an immediate, almost transparent form of discourse was demanded of black writers by the heated temper of the times, a discourse with an immediate end in mind: "At a time like this, scorching irony, not convincing argument, is needed . . . a fiery stream of biting ridicule, blasting reproach, withering sarcasm, and stern rebuke. For it is not light that is needed, but fire; it is not the gentle shower, but thunder. We need the storm, the whirlwind, and the earthquake." Above all else, Douglass concludes, the rhetoric of the literature created by African Americans must, of necessity, be a purposeful rhetoric, its ends targeted at attacking the evils that afflict black people: "The feeling of the nation must be quickened; the conscience of the nation must be roused; the propriety of the nation must be startled; the hypocrisy of the nation must be exposed; and its crimes against God and man must be proclaimed and denounced." And perhaps this was so; nevertheless, we read Douglass's writings today in literature classes not so much for their content but to understand, and marvel at, his sublime mastery of words, words—to paraphrase Calvino—that never finish saying what it is they have to say, not because of their "message" but because of the language in which that message is inextricably enfolded.

There are as many ways to define a classic in the African American tradition as there are in any other tradition, and these ways are legion. So many essays have been published entitled "What Is a Classic?" that they could fill several large anthologies. And while no one can say explicitly why generations of readers return to read certain texts, just about everyone can agree that making a best-seller list in one's lifetime is most certainly not an index of fame or influence over time; the longevity of one's readership—of books about which one says, "I am rereading," as Calvino puts it—on the other hand, most certainly is. So, the size of one's readership (through library use, internet access, and sales) cumulatively is an interesting factor to consider; and because of series such as the Penguin Classics, we can gain a sense, for our purposes, of those texts written by authors in previous generations that have sustained sales—mostly for classroom use—long after their authors were dead.

There can be little doubt that *Narrative of the Life of Frederick Douglass* (1845), *The Souls of Black Folk* (1903), by W. E. B. Du Bois, and *Their Eyes Were Watching God* (1937), by Zora Neale Hurston, are the three most classic of the black classics—again, as measured by consumption—while Langston Hughes's poetry, though not purchased as books in these large numbers, is accessed through the internet as frequently as that of any other American poet, and indeed profoundly more so than most. Within Penguin's Portable Series list, the most popular individual titles, excluding Douglass's first slave narrative and Du Bois's *Souls*, are:

Up from Slavery (1903), Booker T. Washington
The Autobiography of an Ex-Colored Man (1912), James
    Weldon Johnson
God's Trombones (1926), James Weldon Johnson
Passing (1929), Nella Larsen

The Marrow of Tradition (1898), Charles W. Chesnutt
Incidents in the Life of a Slave Girl (1861), Harriet Jacobs
The Interesting Narrative (1789), Olaudah Equiano
The House Behind the Cedars (1900), Charles W. Chesnutt
My Bondage and My Freedom (1855), Frederick Douglass
Quicksand (1928), Nella Larsen

These titles form a canon of classics of African American literature, judged by classroom readership. If we add Jean Toomer's novel *Cane* (1922), arguably the first work of African American modernism, along with Douglass's first narrative, Du Bois's *The Souls*, and Hurston's *Their Eyes*, we would most certainly have included many of the touchstones of black literature published before 1940, when Richard Wright published *Native Son*.

Every teacher's syllabus constitutes a canon of sorts, and I teach these texts and a few others as the classics of the black canon. Why these particular texts? I can think of two reasons: First, these texts signify or riff upon each other, repeating, borrowing, and extending metaphors book to book, generation to generation. To take just a few examples, Equiano's eighteenth-century use of the trope of the talking book (an image found, remarkably, in five slave narratives published between 1770 and 1811) becomes, with Frederick Douglass, the representation of the quest for freedom as, necessarily, the quest for literacy, for a freedom larger than physical manumission; we might think of this as the representation of metaphysical manumission, of freedom and literacy—the literacy of great literature—inextricably intertwined. Douglass transformed the metaphor of the talking book into the trope of chiasmus, a repetition with a stinging reversal: "You have seen how a man becomes a slave, you will see how a slave becomes a man." Du Bois, with Douglass very much on his mind, transmuted chiasmus a half century later into the metaphor of duality or double consciousness, a necessary condition of living one's life, as he memorably put it, behind a "veil."

Du Bois's metaphor has a powerful legacy in twentieth-century black fiction: James Weldon Johnson, in *Ex-Colored*

Man, literalizes the trope of double consciousness by depicting as his protagonist a man who, at will, can occupy two distinct racial spaces, one black, one white, and who moves seamlessly, if ruefully, between them; Toomer's *Cane* takes Du Bois's metaphor of duality for the inevitably split consciousness that every Negro must feel living in a country in which her or his status as a citizen is liminal at best, or has been erased at worst, and makes of this the metaphor for the human condition itself under modernity, a tellingly bold rhetorical gesture— one designed to make the Negro the metaphor of the human condition. And Hurston, in *Their Eyes*, extends Toomer's revision even further, depicting a character who can gain her voice only once she can name this condition of duality or double consciousness and then glide gracefully and lyrically between her two selves, an "inside" self and an "outside" one.

More recently, Alice Walker, in *The Color Purple*, signifies upon two aspects of the narrative strategy of *Their Eyes*: First, she revisits the theme of a young black woman finding her voice, depicting a protagonist who writes herself into being through letters addressed to God and to her sister, Nettie— letters that grow ever more sophisticated in their syntax and grammar and imagery as she comes to consciousness before our very eyes, letter to letter; and second, Walker riffs on Hurston's use of a vernacular-inflected free indirect discourse to show that black English has the capacity to serve as the medium for narrating a novel through the black dialect that forms a most pliable and expansive language in Celie's letters. Ralph Ellison makes Du Bois's metaphor of the veil a trope of blindness and life underground for his protagonist in *Invisible Man*, a protagonist who, as he types the story of his life from a hole underground, writes himself into being in the first person (in contradistinction to Richard Wright's protagonist, Bigger Thomas, whose reactive tale of fear and flight is told in the third person). Walker's novel also riffs on Ellison's claim for the revolutionary possibilities of writing the self into being, whereas Hurston's protagonist, Janie, speaks herself into being. Ellison himself signified multiply upon Richard Wright's *Native Son*, from the title to the use of the first-person bildungs-roman to chart the coming to consciousness of a sensitive protagonist moving from blindness and an inability to do little more than react to his environment, to the insight gained by wresting control of his identity from social forces and strong individuals that would circumscribe and confine his life choices. Toni Morrison, master supernaturalist and perhaps the greatest black novelist of all, trumps Ellison's trope of blindness by returning over and over to the possibilities and limits of insight within worlds confined or circumscribed not by supraforces (à la Wright) but by the confines of the imagination and the ironies of individual and family history, signifying upon Faulkner, Woolf, and García Márquez in the process. And Ishmael Reed, the father of black postmodernism and what we might think of as the hip-hop novel, the tradition's master parodist, signifies upon everybody and everything in the black literary tradition, from the slave narratives to the Harlem Renaissance to black nationalism and feminism.

This sort of literary signifying is what makes a literary tradition, well, a "tradition," rather than a simple list of books whose authors happen to have been born in the same country, share the same gender, or would be identified by their peers as belonging to this ethnic group or that. What makes these books special—"classic"—however, is something else. Each text has the uncanny capacity to take the seemingly mundane details of the day-to-day African American experience of its time and transmute those details and the characters' actions into something that transcends its ostensible subject's time and place, its specificity. These texts reveal the human universal through the African American particular: All true art, all classics, do this; this is what "art" is, a revelation of that which makes each of us sublimely human, rendered in the minute details of the actions and thoughts and feelings of a compelling character embedded in a time and place. But as soon as we find ourselves turning to a text for its anthropological or sociological data, we have left the realm of art; we have reduced the complexity of fiction or poetry to an essay, and this is not what imaginative literature is for. Richard Wright, at his best, did this, as did his signifying disciple Ralph Ellison; Louis

Armstrong and Duke Ellington, Bessie Smith and Billie Holiday achieved this effect in music; Jacob Lawrence and Romare Bearden achieved it in the visual arts. And this is what Wole Soyinka does in his tragedies, what Toni Morrison does in her novels, what Derek Walcott did in his poetry. And while it is risky to name one's contemporaries in a list such as this, I think that Rita Dove and Jamaica Kincaid achieve this effect as well, as do Colson Whitehead and Edwidge Danticat, in a younger generation. (There are other writers whom I would include in this group had I the space.) By delving ever so deeply into the particularity of the African and African American experience, these authors manage, somehow, to come out the other side, making the race or the gender of their characters almost translucent, less important than the fact that they stand as aspects of ourselves beyond race or gender or time or place, precisely in the same magical way that Hamlet never remains for long stuck as a prince in a court in Denmark.

Each classic black text reveals to us, uncannily, subtly, how the Black Experience is inscribed, inextricably and indelibly, in the human experience, and how the human experience takes one of its myriad forms in blackface, as it were. Together, such texts also demonstrate, implicitly, that African American culture is one of the world's truly great and eternal cultures, as noble and as resplendent as any. And it is to publish such texts, written by African and African American authors, that Penguin has created this new series, which I have the pleasure of editing.

HENRY LOUIS GATES, JR.

Introduction

The Mis-education of the Negro (1933) is the most popular text written by Carter G. Woodson, one of the most celebrated and influential African American intellectuals of the twentieth century. "Mis-education" refers to black students' induction into the dominant white curriculum, even as this system of knowledge maligns black history and culture by denying their existence, or by insisting that people of African descent lack a history and culture worthy of respect. Woodson observed that such distortions in knowledge justified and motivated the physical violence black people encountered in the world, declaring, "There would be no lynching if it did not start in the schoolroom." In *Mis-education*, Woodson advocated suspicion of the dominant education system because the ideological orientation of mainstream education was at odds with the interests of black people.

The ideas at the heart of *Mis-education* have resonated across generations, carrying intellectual significance inside and outside of the elite academy. The term "mis-education" functions as a popular shorthand in political discourse, indexing a critique of white supremacy and its embeddedness in schools. *Mis-education* is a seminal and founding text for Black Studies; an inaugural course offered in the black studies department at San Francisco State College—the first of its kind in the country—was titled "The Mis-education of the Negro." Lauryn Hill's 1998 R&B and hip-hop album, *The Miseducation of Lauryn Hill*, which won five Grammy Awards, was a clear nod to Woodson's 1933 treatise.

Though published in 1933, *Mis-education* discussed central

ideas that motivated Woodson's work in the previous decades. Unlike Woodson's previous books, *Mis-education* was composed not only of rigorous scholarly research but of theory grounded by his personal experiences as an educator, student, and researcher, combined with his deep study of the relationship between black people's representation in the system of knowledge undergirding school and their suffering in the world.

A SCHOOLMASTER TO HIS RACE,
1875–1915

Many affectionately refer to Woodson as "the father of black history" because he earned his PhD in history from Harvard in 1912—making him the second African American to do so, after W. E. B. Du Bois—and because he founded Negro History Week in 1926, which is celebrated today as Black History Month. However, Woodson was first and foremost a schoolteacher. Or, as educators and students put it after his death in 1950, he was a "Schoolmaster to His Race." Woodson's identity as a professional schoolteacher played a critical role in shaping the conviction and critiques manifested in *Mis-education*.

Born in Buckingham County, Virginia, in 1875, Woodson began his education in a one-room schoolhouse under the tutelage of his formerly enslaved maternal uncles, John and James Riddle. Woodson balanced school with work on the family farm, but his family instilled in him a deep commitment to education. He excelled in his studies. After learning "the fundamentals" from his uncles, Woodson moved to West Virginia, where he worked in the coal mines before starting high school at the age of twenty. But Woodson stepped into his role as an educator even before he entered high school. As a child, Woodson was responsible for reading newspapers to his formerly enslaved father, James Henry Woodson, who was illiterate. Similarly, a man named Oliver Jones—a coal miner and Civil War veteran who was formerly enslaved—paid Woodson to read to him and a group of illiterate miners in the evenings, after long days of work. This communal literacy taught Woodson how education might serve higher purposes than individual achievement and social mobility. Such informal educational experiences laid the groundwork for his expansive career as a teacher.

Woodson graduated from Frederick Douglass High School in Huntington, West Virginia, in May 1896, which coincided with the landmark Supreme Court ruling of *Plessy v. Ferguson*. Just as Woodson prepared to enter college, as the first in his family to do so, the period of de jure racial segregation, otherwise known as Jim Crow, was legally formalized in the United States. In 1897, Woodson enrolled at Kentucky's Berea College, the only southern college to enroll both black and white students at the time. Woodson taught in public schools while completing the bulk of his studies through correspondence courses.

While still pursuing his degree at Berea, Woodson was hired in 1900 to replace his first cousin Carter Barnett as principal of his alma mater, Douglass High School. Barnett was fired by the white school board because he used his newspaper, *The West Virginia Spokesman*, to advocate for a group of independent black candidates running for political office. Their kinship was likely unknown to local white school leaders. This event reminded Woodson of the various ways school authorities surveilled and targeted black educators when they stepped too far out of line in America's segregated public schools. As he explained three decades later in *Mis-education*, "These teachers . . . are powerless. . . . The education of the Negroes, then, the most important thing in the uplift of the Negroes, is almost entirely in the hands of those who have enslaved them and now segregate them" (20).

Woodson graduated from Berea in 1903 and applied to teach in the Philippines through the US government, where he worked until early 1907. The United States defeated Spain in 1898 during the Spanish-American War, took control of Cuba, Puerto Rico, Guam, and the Philippines, and in 1901 began sending American teachers to transform the education system in this newly "acquired" territory. Reflecting on this experience in *Mis-education*, Woodson described how the majority of teachers sought to impose American ideals and history onto Filipino students. Those educators who leaned into the higher aims of the vocation, however, rejected the books based on American life and made it a point to recognize the distinct history and culture of the local people. Woodson explained, "This real educator taught them about their own hero, José Rizal, who gave his life as a martyr for the freedom of his country" (107). Woodson furthered his education while in the Philippines, completing correspondence courses in Spanish and French at the University of Chicago, where he previously attended summer school in 1902.

Upon leaving the Philippines, Woodson traveled to and studied in various countries in Asia, North Africa, and Europe before returning to the United States in 1907. He continued his studies in Romance languages and history at the University of Chicago, where he earned a second bachelor's and a master's degree in 1908. He then moved to Cambridge, Massachusetts, to begin doctoral studies in Harvard's History Department, twelve years after W. E. B. Du Bois became the first black person to earn a doctorate from Harvard.

Having taught for several years and traveled the world, Woodson struggled with the narrow perspectives of history he encountered. Woodson's original doctoral adviser, Edward Channing, rejected the idea that there was any such thing as Negro history. Channing also believed that black individuals in Africa and America were inferior "in race stamina and race achievement," and accredited any academic accomplishments made by Du Bois, Woodson, and later Charles H. Wesley—the third black PhD in history from Harvard—to their mixed-race ancestry. Woodson switched advisers to Albert Bushnell Hart, who advised Du Bois, likely believing him to be less conservative in his racial politics than Channing. But while Hart was not opposed to black people's educational uplift, he did believe they were an inferior race.[1]

Such antiblack ideas were not limited to Harvard. For instance, Ulrich B. Phillips, who taught at Yale University, shaped the dominant school of thought on the study of slavery in the United States during the first decades of the twentieth century. Phillips praised enslavers, insisting that brutality was of little significance and that, overall, slavery was a positive influence on the black race, given that they descended from Africa, a place he believed to be absent of culture and civilization. Phillips studied under William A. Dunning at Columbia University, who shaped the major school of thought on the period of American Reconstruction, which ultimately justified black disenfranchisement. He insisted that Reconstruction was corrupted by radical Republicans and unqualified African Americans in leadership.[2]

Woodson struggled through his Harvard exams at the end of his first year, and he contemplated giving up on doctoral studies altogether. In 1909, he moved to Washington, DC, to teach in the city's public schools, because Harvard did not offer him funding for his second year. In DC, Woodson studied to retake his exams and conducted research at the Library of Congress while teaching full-time. He completed his degree in 1912, though he faced major challenges with his dissertation committee along the way. Woodson's dissertation, "The Disruption of Virginia," explored the history of the secessionist movement in western Virginia beginning in the early 1700s. Years later, in *The Negro World* newspaper, Woodson shared that it took him twenty years to recover from his education at America's most elite university.

While working on his dissertation, Woodson taught at the M Street School in DC, arguably the most prestigious black high school in the country, at a time when African Americans' access to secondary education was extremely limited. Teaching in DC was just as important to Woodson's intellectual development as his research to complete his doctoral degree. In July 1915, Roscoe Bruce, the assistant superintendent of colored schools in DC, reported that African American teachers had to squeeze in aspects of black history and literature on their own accord, despite the fact that some educators in DC had actually published important books on such topics, including Woodson's *The Education of the Negro Prior to 1861*, published that year. Bruce made the following appeal to local officials: "It gives our children and youth a sense of pride in the stock from which they sprang, an honorable self-confidence, a faith in the future and its possibilities, to know what men and women of Negro blood have actually done, whether in the fields or in the schoolroom or in the war for the building of America."[3]

Across the country, black teachers organized to make their curricula more relevant for students, and they critiqued the studious omission of black life in formal curricula, anticipating many of the ideas appearing in *Mis-education* two decades later. The overrepresentation of white narratives of achievement in curriculum, Woodson argued, exaggerated white people's importance in the history of human progress; it motivated white students to success while demotivating black students or encouraging them to aspire to whiteness and eschew their blackness as African descendant people. For these reasons, Woodson declared, "The education of any people should begin with the people themselves, but Negroes thus trained have been dreaming about the ancients of Europe and about those who have tried to imitate them" (27). Woodson argued that imitation and internalizing a fascination with European and Euro-American culture and values diminished possibilities for a positive black self-image and developing necessary critiques of white supremacy.

In September 1915, Woodson founded the Association for the Study of Negro Life and History with four other African American men at the Wabash Avenue Colored YMCA in Chicago: George C. Hall (physician), Alexander Jackson (executive secretary of Wabash YMCA), William B. Hartgrove (Washington, DC, schoolteacher), and James E. Stamps (Yale graduate student in economics). According to James Stamps, Woodson "pointed out what an organization which would report continuously true historical achievement of the Negro would mean to the old and young." It would play a critical role in "changing the image of the Negro," but it would also "arouse the youth to study for achievement."[4]

Using his small salary as a teacher, Woodson immediately

began growing the association and its work. *The Journal of Negro History* was one of the first steps in establishing the organization's academic credibility. He published the first issue in January 1916, which included articles and essays by numerous DC teachers, including Jessie Fauset, Mary Church Terrell, William Hartgrove, and John W. Cromwell.[5] The ASNLH hosted its first annual conference in 1917, a gathering for scholars and teachers from around the country. In 1921, Woodson established the Associated Publishers, Inc., which published and supported new scholarship on black life and culture. Woodson's association and its academic programming helped expand and sustain what scholar Pero G. Dagbovie has termed "the early black history movement."[6] It is important to note that Woodson's ASNLH served as an institutional forerunner to the formalization of Black Studies in American universities decades later, in the post–Civil Rights era.

THE CHALLENGES OF WHITE PATERNALISM, 1920–1932

In 1919, Woodson transitioned from public schools to join the faculty at Howard University. Woodson made this transition during the Red Summer of 1919, when race riots erupted around the country as soldiers returned home from World War I. Woodson himself witnessed a lynching during the riots in Washington, DC. This experience reinforced his belief that there was a relationship between the debasement of black people in the canons of knowledge and the violence shaping their realities in the material world. In *Mis-education*, Woodson declared, "There would be no lynching if it did not start in the schoolroom. Why not exploit, enslave, or exterminate a class that everybody is taught to regard as inferior?" (8).

At Howard, Woodson stepped into the role as dean of the School of Liberal Arts, professor of history, and head of its graduate faculty. Woodson's "History 30: The Negro in American History" is quite possibly the first course on black history and culture offered in an American university. Indeed, three years before Woodson joined the Howard faculty, the university's white executive committee denied a faculty proposal for a course focused on race. The committee believe it "inexpedient to establish a course in Negro problems at this time."[7] Woodson's course stood in stark contrast to the expansive number of Howard University courses focusing on European history. The objective of "History 30" was to "connect with the movements in our history such factors as slavery, abolition, colonization and the compromises leading up to the conflict of the North and South. It will also treat the status of the free Negro, the program of the Civil War, the drama of Reconstruction, efforts of racial adjustment, and the struggle of the Negro for social justice."[8]

Woodson resigned after one year of intense conflicts with J. Stanley Durkee, the university's white president. Woodson refused Durkee's demand that he monitor his colleagues' attendance in chapel, he offered continuing education courses for black teachers without the president's knowledge, and he publicly critiqued Durkee for removing books he believed to have Communist leanings from Howard's library.[9] Durkee warned that Woodson either write a formal letter of apology for his insubordination or he would be fired. Woodson refused to apologize.[10]

He vented about his frustrations to Jesse Moorland, an early board member of the ASNLH, DC minister, and Howard alum that donated an extensive collection of books that led to the university's research center. Woodson asked Moorland, "If well-educated Negroes cannot remain at Howard University without losing their self-respect, what hope is there for the Negro youth?" (145). In this letter, Woodson named white paternalism as a key impediment to black education. White allies constantly exerted control over black leaders and intellectuals, suggesting that African Americans were unable to make rational or responsible decisions. The critiques outlined in this 1920 letter to Moorland resonate with many of those expressed in *Mis-education* in 1933.

Woodson left Howard and accepted a position as dean at West Virginia State College, where he worked for two years, reorganizing the school's academic program. All the while he was building the ASNLH: growing its membership, editing *The Journal of Negro History*, and publishing books through its publishing arm, the Associated Publishers, Inc. In 1922, Woodson published his first textbook, *The Negro in Our History*, which was widely celebrated among educators, in the black press, and in the historical profession. Woodson was carving out space for "Negro history" as a legitimate field of study, and there was great momentum behind his work. In 1926, Woodson founded Negro History Week, which emerged from an annual celebration he headed up through his fraternity, Omega Psi Phi Fraternity, Inc., beginning in April 1921.[11] By the mid-1930s, the overwhelming majority of black southern schools celebrated Negro History Week, especially the high schools. In 1940, Du Bois referred to Woodson's successful popularization of Negro History Week during the Black Renaissance as "the single greatest accomplishment" in the movement "for the advancement of art and literature."[12]

White philanthropists—such as the Rosenwald Foundation, the Carnegie Corporation, and the Laura Spelman Rockefeller Memorial Fund—and white education reformers, including Thomas Jesse Jones, education director of the Phelps Stokes Fund, supported the ASNLH through its first decade. Their financial support was essential to the foundational years of the organization. All the while, Woodson's insistence on intellectual autonomy and his growing critiques of white control began to damage his reputation among white funders.[13] By the 1930s, Woodson was completely ostracized among this group of philanthropists and reformers. The ASNLH came to rely on smaller donations from a larger number of members—largely black schoolteachers.

Woodson's critiques of white philanthropy helped him confront relationships between colonial education in Africa and white control of black education in the United States. In *Miseducation*, he observed, "The Negro, both in Africa and America, is being turned first here and there experimentally by so-called friends who in the final analysis assist the Negro merely in remaining in the dark" (133–134) Woodson's comparative analysis began in the 1920s but became most explicit by the time *Mis-education* was published. Such ideas position Woodson as a forerunner to scholars who have named black suffering in education as a global practice of white coloniality and empire, such as Aimé Césaire, Sylvia Wynter, and Ngũgĩ wa Thiong'o, among others.

Woodson's standing among white funders became most evident in 1932, when the Phelps Stokes Fund and Thomas Jesse Jones assembled a team of scholars to develop a multivolume encyclopedia on the Negro under the condition that Woodson and Du Bois not be included in the project. After intense pushback from potential contributors, invitations were extended to Woodson and Du Bois. Du Bois thought it practical to accept the invitation and find some middle ground to ensure that intellectual freedom could be maintained. However, Woodson refused. He was outraged and insisted that the project infringed on intellectual work already taken up by the ASNLH. He was also frustrated by Du Bois and the other black scholars for agreeing to the project.

The encyclopedia controversy reflected core arguments at the heart of *Mis-education*. For Woodson, it simply became more evidence that white paternalism and ideological manipulation continued to go hand in hand, and both were deeply ingrained in black schooling at a systemic level.

> Negroes have no control over their education and have little voice in their other affairs pertaining thereto. In a few cases Negroes have been chosen as members of public boards of education, and some have been appointed members of private boards, but these Negroes are always such a small minority that they do not figure in the final working out of the educational program (20).

Woodson understood efforts to control scholarship produced by black academics, as in the case of this encyclopedia, to be directly related to white control of black education at the level of institutions and curriculum.

SITUATING *MIS-EDUCATION* AS AN
AFRICAN AMERICAN CLASSIC

The Mis-education of the Negro was released one year after the encyclopedia controversy. There is no question that the book was, in part, a response to this event. But to be clear, it was also a response to an accumulation of experiences, where Woodson witnessed the suppression of black education as a teacher, student, and institution builder. And his analysis of these experiences was informed by his training as a historian and the distortions of black life he witnessed in historical scholarship.

By 1933, Woodson severed all formal ties to public schools and universities, having fully committed his life to challenging the oppressive realities in black education. By his assessment, the challenges ran much deeper than black schools being starved of resources. He was singularly concerned with the cultural politics of white supremacy, which functioned at the level of ideology and through the system of representation. Woodson's life's work became rewriting the scripts of knowledge to account for the humanity of black people—and in doing so revising what constituted human history altogether.

While many of Woodson's accomplishments are often overlooked in recent times, *Mis-education* has had a lasting impact, both inside and outside of the academy. Ironically, the book is the least scholarly of all of Woodson's writings. Woodson broke loose from rigid conventions of academic scholarship and disciplinary boundaries when writing *Mis-education*, a departure from his usual commitment to scholarly conventions, including the idea of objectivity. With this text, he allowed his heart to inform the substance of his writing.[14]

Mis-education is a work of social criticism that emerged from a deep and profound love for black people. It is an indictment of mainstream American education for its hostilities toward African Americans, in both its policies and curriculum. While it defies any single genre, the book sits in the company of black polemics, alongside works like David Walker's *Appeal to the Coloured Citizens of the World* in 1829 and Harold Cruse's

The Crisis of the Negro Intellectual in 1967. The militant tone of Woodson's plea, that black Americans operate with a heightened level of vigilance when engaging educational programs, places it squarely in this realm of the African American literary tradition.

But the book's discrete focus on the political importance of education in black American life also places it in a tradition of black educational criticism. It is in conversation with such works as Anna Julia Cooper's *A Voice from the South: By a Black Woman from the South* in 1892 and W. E. B. Du Bois's *Souls of Black Folk* in 1903. Woodson insisted that any meaningful education must prioritize the political needs of black people and be set apart from the larger aims of the dominant white American educational agenda. He advocated for an education rooted in a love for black people and their culture, as well as a deep appreciation for their ongoing, persistent human struggle. If those pursuing education "would fall in love with his own people and begin to sacrifice for their uplift—if the 'highly educated' Negro would do these things," Woodson exclaimed, "he could solve some of the problems now confronting the race" (35). Yet miseducation, or the systematic induction of black learners into the dominant systems of knowledge, continued to be an impediment to such action.

Woodson invited educators to reconsider what constitutes knowledge by developing new curricular scripts that rigorously accounted for black life and culture. He especially emphasized this point for humanities and social science education, but he also demanded that educational objectives be tailored to address the material conditions of students' lives and their communities. A central objective of education must be to support students in thinking critically about their sociohistorical realities through disciplined engagement with black American life and culture; their condition required an incisive social analysis of the political structure as antiblack and historically derived. As Woodson wrote in 1934, teachers needed "to show wherein these conditions have resulted from unsound policies and unwise methods."[15]

Woodson's line of argumentation—that antiblackness was embedded in curriculum, which directly informed social behavior in society—was novel philosophical insight for its time. As Black Studies scholar Sylvia Wynter wrote in 1990, theorizing "miseducation" might be thought of as "Woodson's conceptual breakthrough."[16] He gave a name to something that represented a central conflict in black people's struggle for education in service of freedom.

The struggle for black education was about more than access and inclusion. Woodson was primarily concerned with the moral and ideological substance of the education African Americans received when they did gain access. In fact, much of the criticism in *Mis-education* was reserved for those black people who were educated and elevated to positions of leadership in African American communities. To this point, he explained:

> It may be of no importance to the race to be able to boast today of many times as many "educated" members as it had in 1865. If they are of the wrong kind the increase in numbers will be a disadvantage rather than an advantage. The only question which concerns us here is whether these "educated" persons are actually equipped to face the ordeal before them or unconsciously contribute to their own undoing by perpetuating the regime of the oppressor (4).

Just any education would not do. Students, teachers, and leaders needed to be educated in a manner that was accountable to black experiences and lived realities, both past and present. Black people had both a distinct history of racial domination and a valuable and worthy history of resistance. Knowledge derived from these experiences would be central for developing meaningful and liberatory educational programs. These perennial truths outlined in *Mis-education* are what have allowed this text to resonate across generations, positioning it alongside many other African American classics.

THE AFTERLIFE OF WOODSON'S IDEAS

The Mis-education of the Negro continued to circulate well
after Woodson's death in 1950, though this edition is the first
time it is being released by a mainstream publisher. The book's
popularity likely dwindled during the 1950s and early 1960s,
when efforts to desegregate schools became a political priority
for black America, and the arguments forwarded in *Mis-
education* about white supremacy in curriculum and school
structures would do more to weaken arguments for desegrega-
tion and racially mixed schooling than it would to advance the
cause. However, the ideas at the heart of the book surged to
the fore once again during the height of the 1960s black student movement, after historic numbers of black students were
admitted to historically white universities. As one historian
notes, "A jump in Black enrollments came in 1967 and 1968
when new federal policy and the mounting effects of the
civil rights movement modestly increased the numbers of Black
undergraduates. . . . From 1970 to 1974, college enrollments
for African Americans shot up 56 percent, compared to a 15
percent increase for whites."[17] The hostilities black students
encountered on these campuses and the alienation they experienced by the curricula led many students back to Woodson's
critiques. Students across the country demanded Black Studies
departments in American colleges and universities beginning
in 1968.

Responding to intellectual demands of the time, the Associated Publishers released a new edition of *The Mis-education
of the Negro* in 1969. President of the ASNLH, Charles H.
Wesley, and veteran educator and ASNLH staff member Thelma
Perry wrote a new introduction for the text. They observed,
"Black youth seem to be asking for what Woodson wanted."
Woodson's "philosophy was not only sound for him but it is
sound for them, as they make the same demands of administrators for Black Studies, Black Curricula, and Black personnel." African American students' demands in the late 1960s
embodied the heart of Woodson's critiques and reflected a

continuum of black consciousness that challenged historical structures of power and antiblack domination in education.

Mis-education is a text that extends from praxis—from Woodson's thinking as well as his doing. For Woodson "was no mere theorist," as Wesley and Perry wrote. "He was an activist and a pragmatist. He knew that writing alone would be inadequate for the enormity of the need."[18] Thus, Woodson's theoretical ideas are best understood when placed alongside his work on the ground—in communities, in classrooms, in constant intellectual and political struggle, only some of which has been covered in this introduction.

The Mis-education of the Negro is a critical text on the timeline of black political and intellectual thought, and it should be read widely by all who are concerned with educational justice. As I write this introduction, massive legislative campaigns are being waged across the United States to limit how histories of race and racial injustice are taught in schools. Many seek to block intellectual frameworks that directly extend from the legacy of scholars like Woodson and his contemporaries from entering classrooms and textbooks. Just as Woodson's words were relevant in 1933 during the height of Jim Crow, and just as they spoke to the heart of black students' demands for Black Studies in 1968, his words continue to resonate in a particularly powerful way in 2023. One can only hope that Woodson's words might inspire broader understanding about the relationship between our systems of knowledge and the injustice around us. Such clarity about the political nature of education is essential to the freedom work being taken up by so many in our time. And if current trends are any measure of the future, *The Mis-education of the Negro* will continue to be relevant in the years to come.

JARVIS R. GIVENS

NOTES TO THE INTRODUCTION

1. Jacqueline Goggin, *Carter G. Woodson: A Life in Black History*, repr. ed. (Baton Rouge: LSU Press, 1997), 21–26; for extensive coverage of the racist ideas of Woodson's graduate school professors, see Jeffrey Aaron Snyder, *Making Black History: The Color Line, Culture, and Race in the Age of Jim Crow* (Athens: University of Georgia Press, 2018), quotes from Channing 23–24, 176 n. 26.

2. August Meier and Elliott Rudwick, *Black History and the Historical Profession, 1915–1980* (Urbana: University of Illinois Press, 1986), 3–4.

3. Roscoe Bruce, "Report of the Assistant Superintendent in Charge of Colored Schools," Annual Report of the Commissioners of the District of Columbia Year Ended June 30, 1915, Report of the Board of Education, July 1, 1915.

4. James E. Stamps, "The Beginning of the ASNLH," *Negro History Bulletin*, November 1965.

5. Carter G. Woodson, *The Journal of Negro History* 1, no. 1 (1916): Woodson, "Notes," 98; J. R. Fauset, review of *Review of The Haitian Revolution, 1791 to 1804*, by T. G. Steward, 93; W. B. Hartgrove, "The Story of Maria Louise Moore and Fannie M. Richards," 23–33.

6. Pero G. Dagbovie, *The Early Black History Movement, Carter G. Woodson, and Lorenzo Johnston Greene* (Urbana: University of Illinois Press, 2007).

7. Rayford W. Logan, *Howard University: The First Hundred Years 1867–1967* (New York: NYU Press, 1969), 171.

8. "1918–19: Catalog of the Officers and Students of Howard University" (Howard University, January 1, 1918), Howard University Catalogs, no. 45: 106–108.

9. Like many other universities, Howard had a long history of censorship. Faculty and students were also forbidden "to make statements to the public press concerning the policy of the Board or the management of the University without prior consultation with University authorities." Logan, *Howard University*, 167.

10. Logan, *Howard University*, 208; Goggin, *Carter G. Woodson*, 51–52.

11. Herman Dreer, *The History of Omega Psi Phi Fraternity: A Brotherhood of Negro College Men, 1911 to 1939* (Washington, DC: Omega Psi Fraternity, 1940), 152–53.

12. W. E. B. Du Bois, *Dusk of Dawn: An Essay Toward an Autobiography of a Race Concept* (New York: Harcourt, Brace and Company, 1940), 203.

13. Darlene Clark Hine, "Carter G. Woodson, White Philanthropy and Negro Historiography," *The History Teacher* 19, no. 3 (1986): 405–25.

14. Walter Daykin, "Nationalism as Expressed in Negro History," *Social Forces* 13 (1934): 257–63.

15. Carter G. Woodson, "Differentiation in Education with Respect to Races," *The New York Age* (January 27, 1934), 5.

16. Sylvia Wynter, "Textbooks and What They Do: The Conceptual Breakthrough of Carter G. Woodson," in *Do Not Call Us Negro: How "Multicultural" Textbooks Perpetuate Racism* (San Francisco: Aspire, 1990).

17. Martha Biondi, *The Black Revolution on Campus*, repr. ed. (Berkeley: University of California Press, 2014), 4.

18. Carter G. Woodson, Charles H. Wesley, and Thelma D. Perry, "Introduction," in *The Mis-Education of the Negro* (Washington, DC: Associated Publishers, 1969), xxiv, viii.

The Mis-education
of the Negro

FOREWORD

The thoughts brought together in this volume have been expressed in recent addresses and articles written by the author. From time to time persons deeply interested in the point of view therein presented have requested that these comments on education be made available in book form. To supply this demand this volume is given to the public.

In the preparation of the volume the author has not followed in detail the productions upon which most of the book is based. The aim is to set forth only the thought developed in passing from the one to the other. The language in some cases, then, is entirely new; and the work is not a collection of essays. In this way repetition has been avoided except to emphasize the thesis which the author sustains.

CARTER GODWIN WOODSON
Washington, D.C.
January, 1933.

INTRODUCTION

Herein are recorded not opinions but the reflections of one who for forty years has participated in the education of the black, brown, yellow and white races in both hemispheres and in tropical and temperate regions. Such experience, too, has been with students in all grades from the kindergarten to the university. The author, moreover, has traveled around the world to observe not only modern school systems in various countries but to study the special systems set up by private agencies and governments to educate the natives in their colonies and dependencies. Some of these observations, too, have been checked against more recent studies on a later tour.

Discussing herein the mistakes made in the education of the Negro, the writer frankly admits that he has committed some of these errors himself. In several chapters, moreover, he specifically points out wherein he himself has strayed from the path of wisdom. This book, then, is not intended as a broadside against any particular person or class, but it is given as a corrective for methods which have not produced satisfactory results.

The author does not support the once popular view that in matters of education Negroes are rightfully subjected to the will of others on the presumption that these poor people are not large taxpayers and must be content with charitable contributions to their uplift. The author takes the position that the consumer pays the tax, and as such every individual of the social order should be given unlimited opportunity to make the most of himself. Such opportunity, too, should not be determined from without by forces set to direct the proscribed element in a way to redound solely to the good of others but should be determined by the make-up of the Negro himself and by what his environment requires of him.

This new program of uplift, the author contends, should not be decided upon by the trial and error method in the application of devices used in dealing with others in a different situation and at another epoch. Only by careful study of the Negro himself and the life which he is forced to lead can we arrive at the proper procedure in this crisis. The mere imparting of information is not education. Above all things, the effort must result in making a man think and do for himself just as the Jews have done in spite of universal persecution.

In thus estimating the results obtained from the so-called education of the Negro the author does not go to the census figures to show the progress of the race. It may be of no importance to the race to be able to boast today of many times as many "educated" members as it had in 1865. If they are of the wrong kind the increase in numbers will be a disadvantage rather than an advantage. The only question which concerns us here is whether these "educated" persons are actually equipped to face the ordeal before them or unconsciously contribute to their own undoing by perpetuating the regime of the oppressor.

Herein, however, lies no argument for the oft-heard contention that education for the white man should mean one thing and for the Negro a different thing. The element of race does not enter here. It is merely a matter of exercising common sense in approaching people through their environment in order to deal with conditions as they are rather than as you would like to see them or imagine that they are. There may be a difference in method of attack, but the principle remains the same.

"Highly educated" Negroes denounce persons who advocate for the Negro a sort of education different in some respects from that now given the white man. Negroes who have been so long inconvenienced and denied opportunities for development are naturally afraid of anything that sounds like discrimination. They are anxious to have everything the white man has even if it is harmful. The possibility of originality in the Negro, therefore, is discounted one hundred percent to maintain a nominal equality. If the whites decide to take up Mormonism the Negroes must follow their lead. If the whites neglect such a study, then the Negroes must do likewise.

The author, however, does not have such an attitude. He considers the educational system as it has developed both in Europe and America an antiquated process which does not hit the mark even in the case of the needs of the white man himself. If the white man wants to hold on to it, let him do so; but the Negro, so far as he is able, should develop and carry out a program of his own.

The so-called modern education, with all its defects, however, does others so much more good than it does the Negro, because it has been worked out in conformity to the needs of those who have enslaved and oppressed weaker peoples. For example, the philosophy and ethics resulting from our educational system have justified slavery, peonage, segregation, and lynching. The oppressor has the right to exploit, to handicap, and to kill the oppressed. Negroes daily educated in the tenets of such a religion of the strong have accepted the status of the weak as divinely ordained, and during the last three generations of their nominal freedom they have done practically nothing to change it. Their pouting and resolutions indulged in by a few of the race have been of little avail.

No systematic effort toward change has been possible, for, taught the same economics, history, philosophy, literature and religion which have established the present code of morals, the Negro's mind has been brought under the control of his oppressor. The problem of holding the Negro down, therefore, is easily solved. When you control a man's thinking you do not have to worry about his actions. You do not have to tell him not to stand here or go yonder. He will find his "proper place" and will stay in it. You do not need to send him to the back door. He will go without being told. In fact, if there is no back door, he will cut one for his special benefit. His education makes it necessary.

The same educational process which inspires and stimulates

the oppressor with the thought that he is everything and has accomplished everything worth while, depresses and crushes at the same time the spark of genius in the Negro by making him feel that his race does not amount to much and never will measure up to the standards of other peoples. The Negro thus educated is a hopeless liability of the race.

The difficulty is that the "educated Negro" is compelled to live and move among his own people whom he has been taught to despise. As a rule, therefore, the "educated Negro" prefers to buy his food from a white grocer because he has been taught that the Negro is not clean. It does not matter how often a Negro washes his hands, then, he cannot clean them, and it does not matter how often a white man uses his hands he cannot soil them. The educated Negro, moreover, is disinclined to take part in Negro business, because he has been taught in economics that Negroes cannot operate in this particular sphere. The "educated Negro" gets less and less pleasure out of the Negro church, not on account of its primitiveness and increasing corruption, but because of his preference for the seats of "righteousness" controlled by his oppressor. This has been his education, and nothing else can be expected of him.

If the "educated Negro" could go off and be white he might be happy, but only a mulatto now and then can do this. The large majority of this class, then, must go through life denouncing white people because they are trying to run away from the blacks and decrying the blacks because they are not white.

CHAPTER I

THE SEAT OF THE TROUBLE

The "educated Negroes" have the attitude of contempt toward their own people because in their own as well as in their mixed schools Negroes are taught to admire the Hebrew, the Greek, the Latin and the Teuton[1] and to despise the African. Of the hundreds of Negro high schools recently examined by an expert in the United States Bureau of Education only eighteen offer a course taking up the history of the Negro, and in most of the Negro colleges and universities where the Negro is thought of, the race is studied only as a problem or dismissed as of little consequence. For example, an officer of a Negro university, thinking that an additional course on the Negro should be given there, called upon a Negro Doctor of Philosophy of the faculty to offer such work. He promptly informed the officer that he knew nothing about the Negro. He did not go to school to waste his time that way. He went to be educated in a system which dismisses the Negro as a nonentity.

At a Negro summer school two years ago, a white instructor gave a course on the Negro, using for his text a work which teaches that whites are superior to the blacks. When asked by one of the students why he used such a textbook the instructor replied that he wanted them to get that point of view. Even schools for Negroes, then, are places where they must be convinced of their inferiority.

The thought of the inferiority of the Negro is drilled into him in almost every class he enters and in almost every book he studies. If he happens to leave school after he masters the fundamentals, before he finishes high school or reaches college, he will naturally escape some of this bias and may recover in time to be of service to his people.

Practically all of the successful Negroes in this country are of the uneducated type or of that of Negroes who have had no formal education at all. The large majority of the Negroes who have put on the finishing touches of our best colleges are all but worthless in the development of their people. If after leaving school they have the opportunity to give out to Negroes what traducers of the race would like to have it learn such persons may thereby earn a living at teaching or preaching what they have been taught but they never become a constructive force in the development of the race. The so-called school, then, becomes a questionable factor in the life of this despised people.

As another has well said, to handicap a student by teaching him that his black face is a curse and that his struggle to change his condition is hopeless is the worst sort of lynching. It kills one's aspirations and dooms him to vagabondage and crime. It is strange, then, that the friends of truth and the promoters of freedom have not risen up against the present propaganda in the schools and crushed it. This crusade is much more important than the anti-lynching movement, because there would be no lynching if it did not start in the schoolroom. Why not exploit, enslave, or exterminate a class that everybody is taught to regard as inferior?

To be more explicit we may go to the seat of the trouble. Our most widely known scholars have been trained in universities outside of the South. Northern and Western institutions, however, have had no time to deal with matters which concern the Negro especially. They must direct their attention to the problems of the majority of their constituents, and too often they have stimulated their prejudices by referring to the Negro as unworthy of consideration. Most of what these universities have offered as language, mathematics, and science may have served a good purpose, but much of what they have taught as economics, history, literature, religion and philosophy is propaganda and cant that involved a waste of time and misdirected the Negroes thus trained.

And even in the certitude of science or mathematics it has been unfortunate that the approach to the Negro has been borrowed from a "foreign" method. For example, the teaching of arithmetic in the fifth grade in a backward county in Mississippi should mean one thing in the Negro school and a decidedly different thing in the white school. The Negro children, as a rule, come from the homes of tenants and peons who have to migrate annually from plantation to plantation, looking for light which they have never seen. The children from the homes of white planters and merchants live permanently in the midst of calculations, family budgets, and the like, which enable them sometimes to learn more by contact than the Negro can acquire in school. Instead of teaching such Negro children less arithmetic, they should be taught much more of it than the white children, for the latter attend a graded school consolidated by free transportation when the Negroes go to one-room rented hovels to be taught without equipment and by incompetent teachers educated scarcely beyond the eighth grade.

In schools of theology Negroes are taught the interpretation of the Bible worked out by those who have justified segregation and winked at the economic debasement of the Negro sometimes almost to the point of starvation. Deriving their sense of right from this teaching, graduates of such schools can have no message to grip the people whom they have been ill trained to serve. Most of such mis-educated ministers, therefore, preach to benches while illiterate Negro preachers do the best they can in supplying the spiritual needs of the masses.

In the schools of business administration Negroes are trained exclusively in the psychology and economics of Wall Street and are, therefore, made to despise the opportunities to run ice wagons, push banana carts, and sell peanuts among their own people. Foreigners, who have not studied economics but have studied Negroes, take up this business and grow rich.

In schools of journalism Negroes are being taught how to edit such metropolitan dailies as the *Chicago Tribune* and the *New York Times*, which would hardly hire a Negro as a janitor; and when these graduates come to the Negro weeklies for

employment they are not prepared to function in such establishments, which, to be successful, must be built upon accurate knowledge of the psychology and philosophy of the
Negro.

When a Negro has finished his education in our schools,
then, he has been equipped to begin the life of an American-
ized or Europeanized white man, but before he steps from the
threshold of his alma mater he is told by his teachers that he
must go back to his own people from whom he has been estranged by a vision of ideals which in his disillusionment he
will realize that he cannot attain. He goes forth to play his
part in life, but he must be both social and bisocial at the same
time. While he is a part of the body politic, he is in addition to
this a member of a particular race to which he must restrict
himself in all matters social. While serving his country he
must serve within a special group. While being a good American, he must above all things be a "good Negro"; and to perform this definite function he must learn to stay in a "Negro's
place."

For the arduous task of serving a race thus handicapped,
however, the Negro graduate has had little or no training at
all. The people whom he has been ordered to serve have been
belittled by his teachers to the extent that he can hardly find
delight in undertaking what his education has led him to think
is impossible. Considering his race as blank in achievement,
then, he sets out to stimulate their imitation of others. The
performance is kept up a while; but, like any other effort at
meaningless imitation, it results in failure.

Facing this undesirable result, the highly educated Negro
often grows sour. He becomes too pessimistic to be a constructive force and usually develops into a chronic fault-finder
or a complainant at the bar of public opinion. Often when he
sees that the fault lies at the door of the white oppressor whom
he is afraid to attack, he turns upon the pioneering Negro who
is at work doing the best he can to extricate himself from an
uncomfortable predicament.

In this effort to imitate, however, these "educated people"
are sincere. They hope to make the Negro conform quickly to

the standard of the whites and thus remove the pretext for the barriers between the races. They do not realize, however, that even if the Negroes do successfully imitate the whites, nothing new has thereby been accomplished. You simply have a larger number of persons doing what others have been doing. The unusual gifts of the race have not thereby been developed, and an unwilling world, therefore, continues to wonder what the Negro is good for.

These "educated" people, however, decry any such thing as race consciousness; and in some respects they are right. They do not like to hear such expressions as "Negro literature," "Negro poetry," "African art," or "thinking black"; and, roughly speaking, we must concede that such things do not exist. These things did not figure in the courses which they pursued in school, and why should they? "Aren't we all Americans? Then, whatever is American is as much the heritage of the Negro as of any other group in this country."

The "highly educated" contend, moreover, that when the Negro emphasizes these things he invites racial discrimination by recognizing such differentness of the races. The thought that the Negro is one thing and the white man another is the stock-in-trade argument of the Caucasian to justify segregation. Why, then, should the Negro blame the white man for doing what he himself does?

These "highly educated" Negroes, however, fail to see that it is not the Negro who takes this position. The white man forces him to it, and to extricate himself therefrom the Negro leader must so deal with the situation as to develop in the segregated group the power with which they can elevate themselves. The differentness of races, moreover, is no evidence of superiority or of inferiority. This merely indicates that each race has certain gifts which the others do not possess. It is by the development of these gifts that every race must justify its right to exist.

CHAPTER II

HOW WE MISSED THE MARK

How we have arrived at the present state of affairs can be understood only by studying the forces effective in the development of Negro education since it was systematically undertaken immediately after Emancipation. To point out merely the defects as they appear today will be of little benefit to the present and future generations. These things must be viewed in their historic setting. The conditions of today have been determined by what has taken place in the past, and in a careful study of this history we may see more clearly the great theatre of events in which the Negro has played a part. We may understand better what his role has been and how well he has functioned in it.

The idea of educating the Negroes after the Civil War was largely a prompting of philanthropy. Their white neighbors failed to assume this responsibility. These black people had been liberated as a result of a sectional conflict out of which their former owners had emerged as victims. From this class, then, the freedmen could not expect much sympathy or cooperation in the effort to prepare themselves to figure as citizens of a modern republic.

From functionaries of the United States Government itself and from those who participated in the conquest of the secessionists early came the plan of teaching these freedmen the simple duties of life as worked out by the Freedmen's Bureau and philanthropic agencies.[1] When systematized this effort became a program for the organization of churches and schools and the direction of them along lines which had been considered most conducive to the progress of people otherwise circumstanced. Here and there some variation was made in this program in view of the fact that the status of the freedmen in no way paralleled that of their friends and teachers, but such thought was not general. When the Negroes in some way would learn to perform the duties which other elements of the population had prepared themselves to discharge they would be duly qualified, it was believed, to function as citizens of the country.

Inasmuch as most Negroes lived in the agricultural South, moreover, and only a few of them at first acquired small farms there was little in their life which any one of thought could not have easily understood. The poverty which afflicted them for a generation after Emancipation held them down to the lowest order of society, nominally free but economically enslaved. The participation of the freedmen in government for a few years during the period known as the Reconstruction[2] had little bearing on their situation except that they did join with the uneducated poor whites in bringing about certain much-desired social reforms, especially in giving the South its first plan of democratic education in providing for a school system at public expense.

Neither this inadequately supported school system nor the struggling higher institutions of a classical order established about the same time, however, connected the Negroes very closely with life as it was. These institutions were concerned rather with life as they hoped to make it. When the Negro found himself deprived of influence in politics, therefore, and at the same time unprepared to participate in the higher functions in the industrial development which this country began to undergo, it soon became evident to him that he was losing ground in the basic things of life. He was spending his time studying about the things which had been or might be, but he was learning little to help him to do better the tasks at hand. Since the Negroes believed that the causes of this untoward condition lay without the race, migration was attempted, and emigration to Africa was again urged. At this psychological moment came the wave of industrial education[3] which swept the country by storm. The educational authorities in the cities and States throughout the Black Belt began to change the course of study to make the training of the Negro conform to this policy.

The missionary teachers from the North in defense of their idea of more liberal training, however, fearlessly attacked this new educational policy; and the Negroes participating in the same dispute arrayed themselves respectively on one side or the other. For a generation thereafter the quarrel as to whether the Negro should be given a classical or a practical education was the dominant topic in Negro schools and churches throughout the United States. Labor was the most important thing of life, it was argued; practical education counted in reaching that end; and the Negro worker must be taught to solve this problem of efficiency before directing attention to other things.

Others more narrow-minded than the advocates of industrial education, seized upon the idea, feeling that, although the Negro must have some semblance of education, it would be a fine stroke to be able to make a distinction between the training given the Negro and that provided for the whites. Inasmuch as the industrial educational idea rapidly gained ground, too, many Negroes for political purposes began to espouse it; and schools and colleges hoping thereby to obtain money worked out accordingly makeshift provisions for such instruction, although they could not satisfactorily offer it. A few real industrial schools actually equipped themselves for this work and turned out a number of graduates with such preparation.

Unfortunately, however, the affair developed into a sort of battle of words, for in spite of all they said and did the majority of the Negroes, those who did make some effort to obtain an education, did not actually receive either the industrial or the classical education. Negroes attended industrial schools, took such training as was prescribed, and received their diplomas; but few of them developed adequate efficiency to be able to do what they were supposedly trained to do. The schools in which they were educated could not provide for all the experience with machinery which white apprentices trained in factories had. Such industrial education as these Negroes received, then, was merely to master a technique already discarded in progressive centers; and even in less complicated operations of industry these schools had no such facilities as to parallel the numerous processes of factories conducted on the plan of the division of labor. Except what value such training might have in the development of the mind by making practical applications of mathematics and science, then, it was a failure.

The majority of Negro graduates of industrial schools, therefore, have gone into other avenues, and too often into those for which they have had no preparation whatever. Some few who actually prepared for the industrial sphere by self-improvement likewise sought other occupations for the reason that Negroes were generally barred from higher pursuits by trades unions; and, being unable to develop captains of industry to increase the demand for persons in these lines, the Negroes have not opened up many such opportunities for themselves.

During these years, too, the schools for the classical education for Negroes have not done any better. They have proceeded on the basis that every ambitious person needs a liberal education when as a matter of fact this does not necessarily follow. The Negro trained in the advanced phases of literature, philosophy, and politics has been unable to develop far in using his knowledge because of having to function in the lower spheres of the social order. Advanced knowledge of science, mathematics and languages, moreover, has not been much more useful except for mental discipline because of the dearth of opportunity to apply such knowledge among people who were largely common laborers in towns or peons on the plantations. The extent to which such higher education has been successful in leading the Negro to think, which above all is the chief purpose of education, has merely made him more of a malcontent when he can sense the drift of things and appreciate the impossibility of success in visioning conditions as they really are.

It is very clear, therefore, that we do not have in the life of the Negro today a large number of persons who have been benefited by either of the systems about which we have quarreled so long. The number of Negro mechanics and artisans have comparatively declined during the last two generations.

The Negroes do not proportionately represent as many skilled laborers as they did before the Civil War. If the practical education which the Negroes received helped to improve the situation so that it is today no worse than what it is, certainly it did not solve the problem as was expected of it.

On the other hand, in spite of much classical education of the Negroes we do not find in the race a large supply of thinkers and philosophers. One excuse is that scholarship among Negroes has been vitiated by the necessity for all of them to combat segregation and fight to retain standing ground in the struggle of the races. Comparatively few American Negroes have produced creditable literature, and still fewer have made any large contribution to philosophy or science. They have not risen to the heights of black men farther removed from the influences of slavery and segregation. For this reason we do not find among American Negroes a Pushkin, a Gomez, a Geoffrey, a Captein or a Dumas. Even men like Roland Hayes and Henry O. Tanner[4] have risen to the higher levels by getting out of this country to relieve themselves of our stifling traditions and to recover from their education.

CHAPTER III

HOW WE DRIFTED AWAY FROM THE TRUTH

How, then, did the education of the Negro take such a trend? The people who maintained schools for the education of certain Negroes before the Civil War were certainly sincere; and so were the missionary workers who went South to enlighten the freedmen after the results of that conflict had given the Negroes a new status. These earnest workers, however, had more enthusiasm than knowledge. They did not understand the task before them. This undertaking, too, was more of an effort toward social uplift than actual education. Their aim was to transform the Negroes, not to develop them. The freedmen who were to be enlightened were given little thought, for the best friends of the race, ill-taught themselves, followed the traditional curricula of the times which did not take the Negro into consideration except to condemn or pity him.

In geography the races were described in conformity with the program of the usual propaganda to engender in whites a race hate of the Negro, and in the Negroes contempt for themselves. A poet of distinction was selected to illustrate the physical features of the white race, a bedecked chief of a tribe those of the red, a proud warrior the brown, a prince the yellow, and a savage with a ring in his nose the black. The Negro, of course, stood at the foot of the social ladder.

The description of the various parts of the world was worked out according to the same plan. The parts inhabited by the Caucasian were treated in detail. Less attention was given to the yellow people, still less to the red, very little to the brown, and practically none to the black race. Those people who are far removed from the physical characteristics of the Caucasians or who do not materially assist them in the domination or exploitation of others were not mentioned except to be belittled or decried.

From the teaching of science the Negro was likewise eliminated. The beginnings of science in various parts of the Orient were mentioned, but the Africans' early advancement in this field was omitted. Students were not told that ancient Africans of the interior knew sufficient science to concoct poisons for arrowheads, to mix durable colors for paintings, to extract metals from nature and refine them for development in the industrial arts. Very little was said about the chemistry in the method of Egyptian embalming which was the product of the mixed breeds of Northern Africa, now known in the modern world as "colored people."

In the study of language in school pupils were made to scoff at the Negro dialect as some peculiar possession of the Negro which they should despise rather than directed to study the background of this language as a broken-down African tongue—in short to understand their own linguistic history, which is certainly more important for them than the study of French Phonetics or Historical Spanish Grammar. To the African language as such no attention was given except in case of the preparation of traders, missionaries and public functionaries to exploit the natives. This number of persons thus trained, of course, constituted a small fraction hardly deserving attention.

From literature the African was excluded altogether. He was not supposed to have expressed any thought worth knowing. The philosophy in the African proverbs and in the rich folklore of that continent was ignored to give preference to that developed on the distant shores of the Mediterranean. Most missionary teachers of the freedmen, like most men of our time, had never read the interesting books of travel in Africa, and had never heard of the *Tarikh Es-Soudan*.[1]

In the teaching of fine arts these instructors usually started with Greece by showing how that art was influenced from without, but they omitted the African influence which scientists now regard as significant and dominant in early Hellas. They failed to teach the student the Mediterranean Melting Pot with the Negroes from Africa bringing their wares, their ideas and their blood therein to influence the history of Greece, Carthage, and Rome. Making desire father to the thought, our teachers either ignored these influences or endeavored to belittle them by working out theories to the contrary.

The bias did not stop at this point, for it invaded the teaching of the professions. Negro law students were told that they belonged to the most criminal element in the country; and an effort was made to justify the procedure in the seats of injustice where law was interpreted as being one thing for the white man and a different thing for the Negro. In constitutional law the spinelessness of the United States Supreme Court in permitting the judicial nullification of the Fourteenth and Fifteenth Amendments was and still is boldly upheld in our few law schools.

In medical schools Negroes were likewise convinced of their inferiority in being reminded of their role as germ carriers. The prevalence of syphilis and tuberculosis among Negroes was especially emphasized without showing that these maladies are more deadly among the Negroes for the reason that they are Caucasian diseases; and since these plagues are new to Negroes, these sufferers have not had time to develop against them the immunity which time has permitted in the Caucasian. Other diseases to which Negroes easily fall prey were mentioned to point out the race as an undesirable element when this condition was due to the Negroes' economic and social status. Little emphasis was placed upon the immunity of the Negro from diseases like yellow fever and influenza which are so disastrous to whites. Yet, the whites were not considered inferior because of this differential resistance to these plagues.

In history, of course, the Negro had no place in this curriculum. He was pictured as a human being of the lower order, unable to subject passion to reason, and therefore useful only when made the hewer of wood and the drawer of water for others. No thought was given to the history of Africa except so far as it had been a field of exploitation for the Caucasian. You might study the history as it was offered in our system from the elementary school throughout the university, and you would never hear Africa mentioned except in the negative. You would never thereby learn that Africans first domesticated the sheep, goat, and cow, developed the idea of trial by jury, produced the first stringed instruments, and gave the world its greatest boon in the discovery of iron. You would never know that prior to the Mohammedan invasion about 1000 A.D. these natives in the heart of Africa had developed powerful kingdoms which were later organized as the Songhay Empire on the order of that of the Romans and boasting of similar grandeur.

Unlike other people, then, the Negro, according to this point of view, was an exception to the natural plan of things, and he had no such mission as that of an outstanding contribution to culture. The status of the Negro, then, was justly fixed as that of an inferior. Teachers of Negroes in their first schools after Emancipation did not proclaim any such doctrine, but the content of their curricula justified these inferences.

An observer from outside of the situation naturally inquires why the Negroes, many of whom serve their race as teachers, have not changed this program. These teachers, however, are powerless. Negroes have no control over their education and have little voice in their other affairs pertaining thereto. In a few cases Negroes have been chosen as members of public boards of education, and some have been appointed members of private boards, but these Negroes are always such a small minority that they do not figure in the final working out of the educational program. The education of the Negroes, then, the most important thing in the uplift of the Negroes, is almost entirely in the hands of those who have enslaved them and now segregate them.

With "mis-educated Negroes" in control themselves, however, it is doubtful that the system would be very much different from what it is or that it would rapidly undergo change. The Negroes thus placed in charge would be the products of the same system and would show no more conception of the task at hand than do the whites who have educated them and shaped their minds as they would have them function. Negro educators of today may have more sympathy and interest in the race than the whites now exploiting Negro institutions as educators, but the former have no more vision than their competitors. Taught from books of the same bias, trained by Caucasians of the same prejudices or by Negroes of enslaved minds, one generation of Negro teachers after another have served for no higher purpose than to do what they are told to do. In other words, a Negro teacher instructing Negro children is in many respects a white teacher thus engaged, for the program in each case is about the same.

There can be no reasonable objection to the Negro's doing what the white man tells him to do, if the white man tells him to do what is right; but right is purely relative. The present system under the control of the whites trains the Negro to be white and at the same time convinces him of the impropriety or the impossibility of his becoming white. It compels the Negro to become a good Negro for the performance of which his education is ill-suited. For the white man's exploitation of the Negro through economic restriction and segregation the present system is sound and will doubtless continue until this gives place to the saner policy of actual interracial cooperation— not the present farce of racial manipulation in which the Negro is a figurehead. History does not furnish a case of the elevation of a people by ignoring the thought and aspiration of the people thus served.

This is slightly dangerous ground here, however, for the Negro's mind has been all but perfectly enslaved in that he has been trained to think what is desired of him. The "highly educated" Negroes do not like to hear anything uttered against this procedure because they make their living in this way, and they feel that they must defend the system. Few mis-educated Negroes ever act otherwise; and, if they so express themselves, they are easily crushed by the large majority to the contrary so that the procession may move on without interruption.

The result, then, is that the Negroes thus mis-educated are

of no service to themselves and none to the white man. The white man does not need the Negroes' professional, commercial or industrial assistance; and as a result of the multiplication of mechanical appliances he no longer needs them in drudgery or menial service. The "highly educated" Negroes, moreover, do not need the Negro professional or commercial classes because Negroes have been taught that whites can serve them more efficiently in these spheres. Reduced, then, to teaching and preaching, the Negroes will have no outlet but to go down a blind alley, if the sort of education which they are now receiving is to enable them to find the way out of their present difficulties.

CHAPTER IV

EDUCATION UNDER OUTSIDE CONTROL

"In the new program of educating the Negro what would become of the white teachers of the race?" some one recently inquired. This is a simple question requiring only a brief answer. The remaining few Christian workers who went South not so long after the Civil War and established schools and churches to lay the foundation on which we should now be building more wisely than we do, we would honor as a martyred throng. Anathema be upon him who would utter a word derogatory to the record of these heroes and heroines! We would pay high tribute also to unselfish Southerners like Haygood, Curry, Ruffner, Northern, and Vance, and to white men of our time, who believe that the only way to elevate people is to help them to help themselves.[1]

The unfortunate successors of the Northern missionary teachers of Negroes, however, have thoroughly demonstrated that they have no useful function in the life of the Negro. They have not the spirit of their predecessors and do not measure up to the requirements of educators desired in accredited colleges. If Negro institutions are to be as efficient as those for the whites in the South the same high standard for the educators to direct them should be maintained. Negro schools cannot go forward with such a load of inefficiency and especially when the white presidents of these institutions are often less scholarly than Negroes who have to serve under them.

By law and custom the white presidents and teachers of Negro schools are prevented from participating freely in the life of the Negro. They occupy, therefore, a most uncomfortable dual position. When the author once taught in a school with a mixed faculty the white women connected with the institution would bow to him in patronizing fashion when on the campus, but elsewhere they did not see him. A white president of one Negro school never entertains a Negro in his home, preferring to shift such guests to the students' dining-room. Another white president of a Negro college maintains on the campus a guest cottage which Negroes can enter only as servants. Still another such functionary does not allow students to enter his home through the front door. Negroes trained under such conditions without protest become downright cowards, and in life will continue as slaves in spite of their nominal emancipation.

"What different method of approach or what sort of appeal would one make to the Negro child that cannot be made just as well by a white teacher?" some one asked not long ago. To be frank we must concede that there is no particular body of facts that Negro teachers can impart to children of their own race that may not be just as easily presented by persons of another race if they have the same attitude as Negro teachers; but in most cases tradition, race hate, segregation, and terrorism make such a thing impossible. The only thing to do in this case, then, is to deal with the situation as it is.

Yet we should not take the position that a qualified white person should not teach in a Negro school. For certain work which temporarily some whites may be able to do better than the Negroes there can be no objection to such service, but if the Negro is to be forced to live in the ghetto he can more easily develop out of it under his own leadership than under that which is super-imposed. The Negro will never be able to show all of his originality as long as his efforts are directed from without by those who socially proscribe him. Such "friends" will unconsciously keep him in the ghetto.

Herein, however, the emphasis is not upon the necessity for separate systems but upon the need for common-sense schools and teachers who understand and continue in sympathy with those whom they instruct. Those who take the position to the contrary have the idea that education is merely a process of imparting information. One who can give out these things or devise an easy plan for so doing, then, is an educator. In a sense this is true, but it accounts for most of the troubles of the Negro. Real education means to inspire people to live more abundantly, to learn to begin with life as they find it and make it better, but the instruction so far given Negroes in colleges and universities has worked to the contrary. In most cases such graduates have merely increased the number of malcontents who offer no program for changing the undesirable conditions about which they complain. One should rely upon protest only when it is supported by a constructive program.

Unfortunately Negroes who think as the author does and dare express themselves are branded as opponents of interracial cooperation. As a matter of fact, however, such Negroes are the real workers in carrying out a program of interracial effort. Cooperation implies equality of the participants in the particular task at hand. On the contrary, however, the usual way now is for the whites to work out their plans behind closed doors, have them approved by a few Negroes serving nominally on a board, and then employ a white or mixed staff to carry out their program. This is not interracial cooperation. It is merely the ancient idea of calling upon the "inferior" to carry out the orders of the "superior." To express it in post-classic language, as did Jessie O. Thomas,[2] "The Negroes do the 'coing' and the whites the 'operating.'"

This unsound attitude of the "friends" of the Negro is due to the persistence of the medieval idea of controlling underprivileged classes. Behind closed doors these "friends" say you need to be careful in advancing Negroes to commanding positions unless it can be determined beforehand that they will do what they are told to do. You can never tell when some Negroes will break out and embarrass their "friends." After being advanced to positions of influence some of them have been known to run amuck and advocate social equality or demand for their race the privileges of democracy when they should restrict themselves to education and religious development.

It is often said, too, that the time is not ripe for Negroes to take over the administration of their institutions, for they do not have the contacts for raising money; but what becomes of this argument when we remember what Booker T. Washington did for Tuskegee and observe what R. R. Moton and John Hope[3] are doing today? As the first Negro president of Howard University Mordecai W. Johnson has raised more money for that institution among philanthropists than all of its former presidents combined. Furthermore, if, after three generations the Negro colleges have not produced men qualified to administer their affairs, such an admission is an eloquent argument that they have failed ingloriously and should be immediately closed.

Recently some one asked me how I connect my criticism of the higher education of the Negroes with new developments in this sphere and especially with the four universities in the South which are to be made possible by the millions obtained from governments, boards, and philanthropists. I believe that the establishment of these four centers of learning at Washington, Atlanta, Nashville, and New Orleans can be so carried out as to mark an epoch in the development of the Negro race. On the other hand, there is just as much possibility for a colossal failure of the whole scheme. If these institutions are to be the replica of universities like Harvard, Yale, Columbia and Chicago, if the men who are to administer them and teach in them are to be the products of roll-top desk theorists who have never touched the life of the Negro, the money thus invested will be just as profitably spent if it is used to buy peanuts to throw at the animals in a circus.

Some of the thought behind the new educational movement is to provide in the South for educating the Negroes who are now crowding Northern universities, especially the medical schools, many of which will not admit Negroes because of the racial friction in hospital practice. In the rush merely to make special provisions for these "undesirable students," however, the institutions which are to train them may be established on false ideas and make the same blunders of the smaller institutions which have preceded them. It will hardly help a poisoned patient to give him a large dose of poison.

In higher institutions for Negroes, organized along lines required for people differently circumstanced, some few may profit by being further grounded in the fundamentals, others may become more adept in the exploitation of their people, and a smaller number may cross the divide and join the whites in useful service; but the large majority of the products of such institutions will increase rather than diminish the load which the masses have had to carry ever since their emancipation. Such ill-prepared workers will have no foundation upon which to build. The education of any people should begin with the people themselves, but Negroes thus trained have been dreaming about the ancients of Europe and about those who have tried to imitate them.

In a course at Harvard, for example, students were required to find out whether Pericles was justly charged with trying to supplant the worship of Jupiter with that of Juno. Since that time Negroes thus engaged have learned that they would have been much better prepared for work among the Negroes in the Black Belt if they had spent that time learning why John Jasper of "sun-do-move" fame joined with Joshua in contending that the planet stood still "in the middle of the line while he fought the battle the second time."[4]

Talking the other day with one of the men now giving the millions to build the four Negro universities in the South, however, I find that he is of the opinion that accredited institutions can be established in mushroom fashion with theorists out of touch with the people. In other words, you can go almost anywhere and build a three-million-dollar plant, place in charge a white man to do what you want accomplished, and in a short while he can secure or have trained to order the men necessary to make a university. "We want here," he will say, "a man who has his Master's degree in English. Send me another who has his Doctor's degree in sociology, and I can use one more in physics."

Now, experience has shown that men of this type may "fill in," but a university cannot be established with such raw recruits. The author once had some experience in trying to man a college in this fashion, and the result was a story that would make an interesting headline for the newspapers. When Dr. William Rainey Harper was establishing the University of Chicago he called to the headship of the various departments only men who had distinguished themselves in the creative world. Some had advanced degrees, and some had not. Several of them had never done any formal graduate work at all. All of them, however, were men whose thought was moving the world. It may be argued that the Negroes have no such men and must have them trained, but such a thing cannot be forced as we are now doing it. It would be much better to stimulate the development of the more progressive teachers of old than experiment with novices produced by the degradation of higher education.

The degradation of the doctorate especially dawned upon the author the other day more clearly than ever when a friend of his rushed into his office saying, "I have been trying to see you for several days. I have just failed to get a job for which I had been working, and I am told that I cannot expect a promotion until I get my 'darkter's 'gree.'" That is what he called it. He could not even pronounce the words, but he is determined to have his "darkter's 'gree" to get the job in sight.

This shameful status of higher education is due in a large measure to low standards of institutions with a tendency toward the diploma-mill procedure. To get a job or to hold one you go in and stay until they "grind" you out a "darkter's 'gree." And you do not have to worry any further. The assumption is that almost any school will be glad to have you thereafter, and you will receive a large salary.

Investigation has shown, however, that men who have the doctorate not only lose touch with the common people, but they do not do as much creative work as those of less formal education. After having this honor conferred upon them, these so-called scholars often rest on their oars. Few persons have thought of the seriousness of such inertia among men who are put in the lead of things because of meeting statutory requirements of frontier universities which are not on the frontier.

The General Education Board and the Julius Rosenwald Fund have a policy which may be a partial solution of the undeveloped

Negro college instructor's problem. These foundations are giving Negro teachers scholarships to improve themselves for work in the sphere in which they are now laboring in the South. These boards, as a rule, do not send one to school to work for the Doctor's degree. If they find a man of experience and good judgment, showing possibilities for growth, they will provide for him to study a year or more to refresh his mind with whatever there is new in his field. Experience has shown that teachers thus helped have later done much better work than Doctors of Philosophy made to order.

The Northern universities, moreover, cannot do graduate work for Negroes along certain lines when they are concentrating on the educational needs of people otherwise circumstanced. The graduate school for Negroes studying chemistry is with George W. Carver at Tuskegee. At least a hundred youths should wait daily upon the words of this scientist to be able to pass on to the generations unborn his great knowledge of agricultural chemistry. Negroes desiring to specialize in agriculture should do it with workers like T. M. Campbell and B. F. Hubert[5] among the Negro farmers of the South.

In education itself the situation is the same. Neither Columbia nor Chicago can give an advanced course in Negro rural education, for their work in education is based primarily upon what they know of the educational needs of the whites. Such work for Negroes must be done under the direction of the trail blazers who are building school houses and reconstructing the educational program of those in the backwoods. Leaders of this type can supply the foundation upon which a university of realistic education may be established.

We offer no argument here against earning advanced degrees, but these should come as honors conferred for training crowned with scholastic distinction, not to enable a man to increase his salary or find a better paying position. The schools which are now directing attention exclusively to these external marks of learning will not contribute much to the uplift of the Negro.

In Cleveland not long ago the author found at the Western Reserve University something unusually encouraging. A native of Mississippi, a white man trained in a Northern university and now serving as a professor in one, has under him in sociology a Negro student from Georgia. For his dissertation this Negro is collecting the sayings of his people in everyday life—their morning greetings, their remarks about the weather, their comments on things which happen around them, their reactions to things which strike them as unusual, and their efforts to interpret life as the panorama passes before them. This white Mississippian and black Georgian are on the right way to understand the Negro and, if they do not fall out about social equality, they will serve the Negro much better than those who are trying to find out whether Henry VIII lusted more after Anne Boleyn than after Catherine of Aragon or whether Elizabeth was justly styled as more untruthful than Philip II of Spain.

CHAPTER V

THE FAILURE TO LEARN TO MAKE A LIVING

The greatest indictment of such education as Negroes have received, however, is that they have thereby learned little as to making a living, the first essential in civilization. Rural Negroes have always known something about agriculture, and in a country where land is abundant they have been able to make some sort of living on the soil even though they have not always employed scientific methods of farming. In industry where the competition is keener, however, what the Negro has learned in school has had little bearing on the situation, as pointed out above. In business the role of education as a factor in the uplift of the Negro has been still less significant. The Negroes of today are unable to employ one another, and the whites are inclined to call on Negroes only when workers of their own race have been taken care of. For the solution of this problem the "mis-educated" Negro has offered no remedy whatever.

What Negroes are now being taught does not bring their minds into harmony with life as they must face it. When a Negro student works his way through college by polishing shoes he does not think of making a special study of the science underlying the production and distribution of leather and its products that he may some day figure in this sphere. The Negro boy sent to college by a mechanic seldom dreams of learning mechanical engineering to build upon the foundation his father has laid that in years to come he may figure as a contractor or a consulting engineer. The Negro girl who goes to college hardly wants to return to her mother if she is a washerwoman, but this girl should come back with sufficient knowledge of physics and chemistry and business administration to use her mother's work as a nucleus for a modern steam laundry. A white professor of a university recently resigned his position to become rich by running a laundry for Negroes in a Southern city. A Negro college instructor would have considered such a suggestion an insult. The so-called education of Negro college graduates leads them to throw away opportunities which they have and to go in quest of those which they do not find.

In the case of the white youth in this country, they can choose their courses more at random and still succeed because of numerous opportunities offered by their people, but even they show so much more wisdom than do Negroes. For example, a year or two after the author left Harvard he found out West a schoolmate who was studying wool. "How did you happen to go into this sort of thing?" the author inquired. His people, the former replied, had had some experience in wool, and in college he prepared for this work. On the contrary, the author studied Aristotle, Plato, Marsiglio of Padua, and Pascasius Rathbertus when he was in college. His friend who studied wool, however, is now independently rich and has sufficient leisure to enjoy the cultural side of life which his knowledge of the science underlying his business developed, but the author has to make his living by begging for a struggling cause.

An observer recently saw at the market near his office a striking example of this inefficiency of our system. He often goes over there at noon to buy a bit of fruit and to talk with a young woman who successfully conducts a fruit stand there in cooperation with her mother. Some years ago he tried to teach her in high school; but her memory was poor, and she could not understand what he was trying to do. She stayed a few weeks, smiling at the others who toiled, and finally left to assist her mother in business. She learned from her mother, however, how to make a living and be happy.

This observer was reminded of this young woman soon thereafter when there came to visit him a friend who succeeded in mastering everything taught in high school at that time and later distinguished himself in college. This highly educated man brought with him a complaint against life. Having had extreme difficulty in finding an opportunity to do what he is trained to do, he has thought several times of committing suicide. A friend encouraged this despondent man to go ahead and do it. The sooner the better. The food and air which he is now consuming may then go to keep alive some one who is in touch with life and able to grapple with its problems. This man has been educated away from the fruit stand.

This friend had been trying to convince this misfit of the unusual opportunities for the Negroes in business, but he reprimanded his adviser for urging him to take up such a task when most Negroes thus engaged have been failures.

"If we invest our money in some enterprise of our own," said he, "those in charge will misuse or misappropriate it. I have learned from my study of economics that we had just as well keep on throwing it away."

Upon investigation, however, it was discovered that this complainant and most others like him have never invested anything in any of the Negro enterprises, although they have tried to make a living by exploiting them. But they feel a bit guilty on this account, and when they have some apparent ground for fault-finding they try to satisfy their conscience which all but condemns them for their suicidal course of getting all they can out of the race while giving nothing back to it.

Gossiping and scandal-mongering Negroes, of course, come to their assistance. Mis-educated by the oppressors of the race, such Negroes expect the Negro business man to fail anyway. They seize, then, upon unfavorable reports, exaggerate the situation, and circulate falsehoods throughout the world to their own undoing. You read such headlines as GREATEST NEGRO BUSINESS FAILS, NEGRO BANK ROBBED BY ITS OFFICERS, and THE TWILIGHT OF NEGRO BUSINESS. The mis-educated Negroes, then, stand by saying:

"I told you so. Negroes cannot run business. My professors pointed that out to me years ago when I studied economics in college; and I never intend to put any of my money in any Negro enterprise."

Yet, investigation shows that in proportion to the amount of capital invested Negro enterprises manifest about as much strength as businesses of others similarly situated. Negro business men have made mistakes, and they are still making them; but the weak link in the chain is that they are not properly supported and do not always grow strong enough to pass through a crisis. The Negro business man, then, has not failed so much as he has failed to get support of Negroes who should be mentally developed sufficiently to see the wisdom of supporting such enterprises.

Now the "highly educated" Negroes who have studied economics at Harvard, Yale, Columbia, and Chicago, will say that the Negro cannot succeed in business because their professors who have never had a moment's experience in this sphere have written accordingly. The whites, they say, have the control of the natural resources and so monopolize the production of raw materials as to eliminate the competition of the Negro. Apparently this is true. All things being equal from the point of view of the oppressor, he sees that the Negro cannot meet the test.

The impatient, "highly educated" Negroes, therefore, say that since under the present system of capitalism the Negro has no chance to toil upward in the economic sphere, the only hope for bettering his condition in this respect is through socialism, the overthrow of the present economic régime, and the inauguration of popular control of resources and agencies which are now being operated for personal gain. This thought is gaining ground among Negroes in this country, and it is rapidly sweeping them into the ranks of what are commonly known as "Communists."

There can be no objection to this radical change, if it brings with it some unselfish genius to do the task better than it is now being done under the present regime of competition. Russia so far has failed to do well this particular thing under a proletarian dictatorship in an agricultural country. But whether this millennium comes or not, the capitalistic system is so strongly intrenched at present that the radicals must struggle many years to overthrow it; and if the Negro has to wait until that time to try to improve his condition he will be starved out so soon that he will not be here to tell the story. The Negro, therefore, like all other oppressed people, must learn to do the so-called "impossible."

The "uneducated" Negro business man, however, is actually at work doing the very thing which the "mis-educated" Negro has been taught to believe cannot be done. This much-handicapped Negro business man could do better if he had some assistance, but our schools are turning out men who do as much to impede the progress of the Negro in business as they do to help him. The trouble is that they do not think for themselves.

If the "highly educated" Negro would forget most of the untried theories taught him in school, if he could see through the propaganda which has been instilled into his mind under the pretext of education, if he would fall in love with his own people and begin to sacrifice for their uplift—if the "highly educated" Negro would do these things, he could solve some of the problems now confronting the race.

During recent years we have heard much of education in business administration departments in Negro colleges; but if they be judged by the products turned out by these departments they are not worth a "continental."[1] The teachers in this field are not prepared to do the work, and the trustees of our institutions are spending their time with trifles instead of addressing themselves to the study of a situation which threatens the Negro with economic extermination.

Recently the author saw the need for a change of attitude when a young woman came almost directly to his office after her graduation from a business school to seek employment. After hearing her story he finally told her that he would give her a trial at fifteen dollars a week.

"Fifteen dollars a week!" she cried, "I cannot live on that, sir."

"I do not see why you cannot," he replied. "You have lived for some time already, and you say that you have never had permanent employment, and you have none at all now."

"But a woman has to dress and to pay board," said she; "and how can she do it on such a pittance?"

The amount offered was small, but it was a great deal more than she is worth at present. In fact, during the first six or nine months of her connection with some enterprise it will be of more service to her than she will be to the firm. Coming out of school without experience, she will be a drag on a business until she learns to discharge some definite function in it. Instead of requiring the firm to pay her she should pay it for training her. Negro business today, then, finds the "miseducated employees" its heaviest burden. Thousands of graduates of white business schools spend years in establishments in undergoing apprenticeship without pay and rejoice to have the opportunity thus to learn how to do things.

The schools in which Negroes are now being trained, however, do not give our young people this point of view. They may occasionally learn the elements of stenography and accounting, but they do not learn how to apply what they have studied. The training which they undergo gives a false conception of life when they believe that the business world owes them a position of leadership. They have the idea of business training that we used to have of teaching when it was thought that we could teach anything we had studied.

Graduates of our business schools lack the courage to throw themselves upon their resources and work for a commission. The large majority of them want to be sure of receiving a certain amount at the end of the week or month. They do not seem to realize that the great strides in business have been made by paying men according to what they do. Persons with such false impressions of life are not good representatives of schools of business administration.

Not long ago a firm of Washington, D.C., appealed to the graduates of several of our colleges and offered them an inviting proposition on the commission basis, but only five of the hundreds appealed to responded and only two of the five gave satisfaction. Another would have succeeded, but he was not honest in handling money because he had learned to purloin the treasury of the athletic organization while in college. All of the others, however, were anxious to serve somewhere in an office for a small wage a week.

Recently one of the large insurance companies selected for special training in this line fifteen college graduates of our accredited institutions and financed their special training in insurance. Only one of the number, however, rendered efficient service in this field. They all abandoned the effort after a few days' trial and accepted work in hotels and with the Pullman Company, or they went into teaching or something else with a fixed stipend until they could enter upon the practice of professions. The thought of the immediate reward, shortsightedness, and the lack of vision and courage to struggle and win the fight made them failures to begin with. They are unwilling to throw aside their coats and collars and do the groundwork of Negro business and thus make opportunities for themselves instead of begging others for a chance.

The educated Negro from the point of view of commerce and industry, then, shows no mental power to understand the situation which he finds. He has apparently read his race out of that sphere, and with the exception of what the illiterate Negroes can do blindly the field is left wide open for foreign exploitation. Foreigners see this opportunity as soon as they reach our shores and begin to manufacture and sell to Negroes especially such things as caps, neckties, and housedresses which may be produced at a small cost and under ordinary circumstances. The main problem with the Negro in this field, however, is salesmanship; that is where he is weak.

It is unfortunate, too, that the educated Negro does not understand or is unwilling to start small enterprises which make the larger ones possible. If he cannot proceed according to the methods of the gigantic corporations about which he reads in books, he does not know how to take hold of things and organize the communities of the poor along lines of small businesses. Such training is necessary, for the large majority of Negroes conducting enterprises have not learned business methods and do not understand the possibilities of the field in which they operate. Most of them in the beginning had had no experience, and started out with such knowledge as they could acquire by observing some one's business from the outside. One of them, for example, had waited on a white business club in passing the members a box of cigars or bringing a pitcher of water. When they began to discuss business, however, he had to leave the room. About the only time he could see them in action was when they were at play, indulging in extravagances which the Negro learned to take up before he could afford them.

Negro businesses thus handicapped, therefore, have not developed stability and the capacity for growth. Practically all worthwhile Negro businesses which were flourishing in 1900 are not existing today. How did this happen? Well, Negro business men have too much to do. They have not time to read the business literature and study the market upon which they depend, and they may not be sufficiently trained to do these things. They are usually operating in the dark or by the hit-or-miss method. They cannot secure intelligent guidance because the schools are not turning out men properly trained to take up Negro business as it is to develop and make it what it ought to be rather than find fault with it. Too often when the founder dies, then, the business dies with him; or it goes to pieces soon after he passes away, for nobody has come into sufficiently close contact with him to learn the secret of his success in spite of his handicaps.

The business among Negroes, too, continues individualistic in spite of advice to the contrary. The founder does not take kindly to the cooperative plan, and such business education as we now give the youth does not make their suggestions to this effect convincing. If the founder happens to be unusually successful, too, the business may outgrow his knowledge, and becoming too unwieldy in his hands, may go to pieces by errors of judgment; or because of mismanagement it may go into the hands of whites who are usually called in at the last hour to do what they call refinancing but what really means the actual taking over of the business from the Negroes. The Negroes, then, finally withdraw their patronage because they realize that it is no longer an enterprise of the race, and the chapter is closed.

All of the failures of the Negro business, however, are not due to troubles from without. Often the Negro business man lacks common sense. The Negro in business, for example, too easily becomes a social "lion." He sometimes plunges into the leadership in local matters. He becomes popular in restricted circles, and men of less magnetism grow jealous of his inroads. He learns how richer men of other races waste money. He builds a finer home than anybody else in the community, and in his social program he does not provide for much contact with the very people upon whom he must depend for patronage. He has the finest car, the most expensive dress, the best summer home, and so far outdistances his competitors in society that they often set to work in child-like fashion to bring him down to their level.

CHAPTER VI

THE EDUCATED NEGRO
LEAVES THE MASSES

One of the most striking evidences of the failure of higher education among Negroes is their estrangement from the masses, the very people upon whom they must eventually count for carrying out a program of progress. Of this the Negro churches supply the most striking illustration. The large majority of Negro communicants still belong to these churches, but the more education the Negroes undergo the less comfort they seem to find in these evangelical groups. These churches do not measure up to the standard set by the university preachers of the Northern centers of learning. Most Negroes returning as finished products from such institutions, then, are forever lost to the popular Negro churches. The unchurched of this class do not become members of such congregations, and those who have thus connected themselves remain chiefly for political or personal reasons and tend to become communicants in name only.

The Negro church, however, although not a shadow of what it ought to be, is the great asset of the race. It is a part of the capital that the race must invest to make its future. The Negro church has taken the lead in education in the schools of the race, it has supplied a forum for the thought of the "highly educated" Negro, it has originated a large portion of the business controlled by Negroes, and in many cases it has made it possible for Negro professional men to exist. It is unfortunate, then, that these classes do not do more to develop the institution. In thus neglecting it they are throwing away what they have, to obtain something which they think they need. In many respects, then, the Negro church during recent generations has become corrupt. It could be improved, but those Negroes who can help the institution have deserted it to exploiters, grafters, and libertines. The "highly educated" Negroes have turned away from the people in the churches, and the gap between the masses and the "talented tenth" is rapidly widening.[1]

Of this many examples may be cited. When the author recently attended in Washington, D.C., one of the popular Negro churches with a membership of several thousands he saw a striking case in evidence. While sitting there he thought of what a power this group could become under the honest leadership of intelligent men and women. Social uplift, business, public welfare—all have their possibilities there if a score or more of our "highly educated" Negroes would work with these people at that center. Looking carefully throughout the audience for such persons, however, he recognized only two college graduates, Kelly Miller and himself; but the former had come to receive from the church a donation to the Community Chest, and the author had come according to appointment to make an appeal in behalf of Miss Nannie H. Burroughs' school.[2] Neither one had manifested any interest in that particular church. This is the way most of them receive attention from our "talented tenth."

Some "highly educated" Negroes say that they have not lost their interest in religion, that they have gone into churches with a more intellectual atmosphere in keeping with their new thoughts and aspirations. And then there is a sort of contagious fever which takes away from the churches of their youth others of less formal education. Talking with a friend from Alabama, the other day, the author found out that after her father had died and she had moved to Washington she forsook the Baptist church in which he had been a prominent worker and joined a ritualistic church which is more fashionable.

Such a change of faith is all right in a sense, for no sensible person today would dare to make an argument in favor of any particular religion. Religion is but religion, if the people live up to the faith they profess. What is said here with respect to the popular churches of Negroes, which happen to be chiefly Methodist and Baptist, would hold also if they were mainly Catholic and Episcopal, provided the large majority of Negroes belonged to those churches. The point here is that the ritualistic churches into which these Negroes have gone do not touch the masses, and they show no promising future for racial development. Such institutions are controlled by those who offer the Negroes only limited opportunity and then sometimes on the condition that they be segregated in the court of the gentiles outside of the temple of Jehovah.

How an "educated Negro" can thus leave the church of his people and accept such Jim-Crowism has always been a puzzle. He cannot be a thinking man. It may be a sort of slave psychology which causes this preference for the leadership of the oppressor. The excuse sometimes given for seeking such religious leadership is that the Negro evangelical churches are "fogy,"[3] but a thinking man would rather be behind the times and have his self-respect than compromise his manhood by accepting segregation. They say that in some of the Negro churches bishoprics are actually bought, but it is better for the Negro to belong to a church where one can secure a bishopric by purchase than be a member of one which would deny the promotion on account of color.

With respect to developing the masses, then, the Negro race has lost ground in recent years. In 1880 when the Negroes had begun to make themselves felt in teaching, the attitude of the leaders was different from what it is today. At that time men went off to school to prepare themselves for the uplift of a downtrodden people. In our time too many Negroes go to school to memorize certain facts to pass examinations for jobs. After they obtain these positions they pay little attention to humanity. This attitude of the "educated Negro" toward the masses results partly from the general trend of all persons toward selfishness, but it works more disastrously among the Negroes than among the whites because the lower classes of the latter have had so much more opportunity.

For some time the author has been making a special study of

the Negroes in the City of Washington to compare their condition of today with that of the past. Now although the "highly educated" Negroes of the District of Columbia have multiplied and apparently are in better circumstances than ever, the masses show almost as much backwardness as they did in 1880. Sometimes you find as many as two or three store-front churches in a single block where Negroes indulge in heathen-like practices which could hardly be equaled in the jungle. The Negroes in Africa have not descended to such depths. Although born and brought up in the Black Belt of the South the author never saw there such idolatrous tendencies as he has seen under the dome of the Capitol.

Such conditions show that the undeveloped Negro has been abandoned by those who should help him. The educated white man, said an observer recently, differs from the "educated Negro" who so readily forsakes the belated element of his race. When a white man sees persons of his own race tending downward to a level of disgrace he does not rest until he works out some plan to lift such unfortunates to higher ground; but the Negro forgets the delinquents of his race and goes his way to feather his own nest, as he has done in leaving the masses in the popular churches.

This is sad indeed, for the Negro church is the only institution the race controls. With the exception of the feeble efforts of a few all but starved-out institutions, the education of the Negroes is controlled by the other element; and save the dramatization of practical education by Booker T. Washington, Negroes have not influenced the system at all in America. In business, the lack of capital, credit, and experience has prevented large undertakings to accumulate the wealth necessary for the ease and comfort essential to higher culture.

In the church, however, the Negro has had sufficient freedom to develop this institution in his own way; but he has failed to do so. His religion is merely a loan from the whites who have enslaved and segregated the Negroes; and the organization, though largely an independent Negro institution, is dominated by the thought of the oppressors of the race. The "educated" Negro minister is so trained as to drift away from the masses and the illiterate preachers into whose hands the people inevitably fall are unable to develop a doctrine and procedure of their own. The dominant thought is to make use of the dogma of the whites as means to an end. Whether the system is what it should be or not it serves the purpose.

In chameleon-like fashion the Negro has taken up almost everything religious which has come along instead of thinking for himself. The English split off from the Catholics because Henry VIII had difficulty in getting sanction from the Church to satisfy his lust for amorous women, and Negroes went with this ilk, singing "God save the King." Others later said the thing necessary is baptism by immersion; and the Negroes joined them as Baptists. Another circle of promoters next said we must have a new method of doing things and we shall call ourselves Methodists; and the Negroes, then, embraced that faith. The Methodists and Baptists split up further on account of the custom of holding slaves; and the Negroes arrayed themselves on the respective sides. The religious agitators divided still more on questions beyond human power to understand; and the Negroes started out in similar fashion to imitate them.

For example, thirty of the two hundred and thirteen religious bodies reported in 1926 were exclusively Negro, while thirty which were primarily white denominations had one or more Negro churches among their number. In other words, Negroes have gone into practically all sects established by the whites; and, in addition to these, they have established thirty of their own to give the system further complication and subdivision. The situation in these churches is aggravated, too, by having too many ministers and about five times as many supervisory officials as a church embracing all Negro communicants would actually need. All of the Negro Methodists in the world, if united, would not need more than twelve bishops, and these would have time to direct the affairs of both Methodists and Baptists in a united church. There is no need for three or four bishops, each teaching the same faith and practice while duplicating the work of the other in the same area merely because a long time ago somebody following the ignorant oppressors of the race in these churches committed the sin of dissension and strife. For all of this unnecessary expense impoverished Negroes have to pay.

The "theology" of "foreigners," too, is the important factor in this disunion of churches and the burden which they impose on an unenlightened people. Theologians have been the "bane of bliss and source of woe." While bringing the joy of conquest to their own camp they have confused the world with disputes which have divided the church and stimulated division and subdivision to the extent that it no longer functions as a Christian agency for the uplift of all men.

To begin with, theology is of pagan origin. Albert Magnus and Thomas Aquinas worked out the first system of it by applying to religious discussion the logic of Aristotle, a pagan philosopher, who believed neither in the creation of the world nor the immortality of the soul. At best it was degenerate learning, based upon the theory that knowledge is gained by the mind working upon itself rather than upon matter or through sense perception. The world was, therefore, confused with the discussion of absurdities as it is today by those of prominent churchmen. By their peculiar "reasoning," too, theologians have sanctioned most of the ills of the ages. They justified the Inquisition, serfdom, and slavery. Theologians of our time defend segregation and the annihilation of one race by the other. They have drifted away from righteousness into an effort to make wrong seem to be right.

While we must hold the Negroes responsible for following these ignorant theorists, we should not charge to their account the origination of this nonsense with which they have confused thoughtless people. As said above, the Negro has been so busy doing what he is told to do that he has not stopped long enough to think about the meaning of these things. He has borrowed the ideas of his traducers instead of delving into things and working out some thought of his own. Some Negro leaders of these religious factions know better, but they hold their following by keeping the people divided, in emphasizing nonessentials the insignificance of which the average man may not appreciate. The "highly educated" Negroes who know better than to follow these unprincipled men have abandoned these popular churches.

While serving as the avenue of the oppressor's propaganda, the Negro church, although doing some good, has prevented the union of diverse elements and has kept the race too weak to overcome foes who have purposely taught Negroes how to quarrel and fight about trifles until their enemies can overcome them. This is the keynote to the control of the so-called inferior races by the self-styled superior. The one thinks and plans while the other in excited fashion seizes upon and destroys his brother with whom he should cooperate.

CHAPTER VII

DISSENSION AND WEAKNESS

In recent years the churches in enlightened centers have devoted less attention to dissension than formerly, but in the rural districts and small cities they have not changed much; and neither in urban communities nor in the country has any one succeeded in bringing these churches together to work for their general welfare. The militant sects are still fighting one another, and in addition to this the members of these sects are contending among themselves. The spirit of Christ cannot dwell in such an atmosphere.

Recent experiences show that these dissensions are about as rank as ever. For example, a rural community, in which an observer spent three weeks a year ago, has no church at all, although eight or ten families live there. No church can thrive among them because, with one or two exceptions, each family represents a different denomination, and the sectarian bias is so pronounced that one will not accept the procedure of the other. Each one loves his fellow man if he thinks as he does; but if his fellow man does not, he hates and shuns him.

In another rural community where the same observer recently spent two weeks he found a small and poorly attended Methodist church. Worshipping there one Sunday morning, he counted only four persons who lived in the community. Others might have come, for there was no other church for them in that place; but this particular church was not of their faith, and their number was too small to justify the establishment of one to their liking. The support given the unfortunate pastor there is so meager that he can hardly afford to come to them once a month, and consequently these peasants are practically without spiritual leadership. People who are so directed as to develop such an attitude are handicapped for life.

Some one recently inquired as to why the religious schools do not teach the people how to tolerate differences of opinion and to cooperate for the common good. This, however, is the thing which these institutions have refused to do. Religious schools have been established, but they are considered necessary to supply workers for denominational outposts and to keep alive the sectarian bias by which the Baptists hope to outstrip the Methodists or the latter the former. No teacher in one of these schools has advanced a single thought which has become a working principle in Christendom, and not one of these centers is worthy of the name of a school of theology. If one would bring together all of the teachers in such schools and carefully sift them he would not find in the whole group a sufficient number qualified to conduct one accredited school of religion. The large majority of them are engaged in imparting to the youth worn-out theories of the ignorant oppressor.

This lack of qualified teachers in Negro schools of theology, however, is not altogether the fault of the teachers themselves. It is due largely to the system to which they belong. Their schools of "theology" are impoverished by their unnecessary multiplication, and consequently the instructors are either poorly paid or not compensated at all. Many of them have to farm, conduct enterprises, or pastor churches to make a living while trying to teach. Often, then, only the inefficient can be retained under such circumstances. Yet those who see how they have failed because of these things nevertheless object to the unification of the churches as taught by Jesus of Nazareth, whom they have all but ceased to follow because of their sectarian bias obtained from thumb-worn books of misguided Americans and Europeans.

Recently an observer saw a result of this in the sermon of a Negro college graduate, trying to preach to a church of the masses. He referred to all the great men in the history of a certain country to show how religious they were, whether they were or not. When he undertook to establish the Christian character of Napoleon, however, several felt like leaving the place in disgust. The climax of the service was a prayer by another "mis-educated" Negro who devoted most of the time to thanking God for Cicero and Demosthenes. Here, then, was a case of the religion of the pagan handed down by the enslaver and segregationist to the Negro.

Returning from the table where he had placed his offering in a church on a Sunday morning not long thereafter, this observer saw another striking example of this failure to hit the mark. He stopped to inquire of his friend, Jim Minor, as to why he had not responded to the appeal for a collection.

"What!" said Jim, "I ain't givin' that man nothing. That man ain't fed me this morning, and I ain't feedin' him."

This was Jim's reaction to a "scholarly" sermon entitled "The Humiliation of the Incarnation." During the discourse, too, the minister had had much to say about John Knox Orthodox, and another of the communicants bowing at that shrine inquired of the observer later as to who this John Knox Orthodox was and where he lived. The observer could not answer all of the inquiries thus evoked, but he tried to explain the best he could that the speaker had "studied" history and theology.

This was the effect this sermon had on an earnest congregation. The minister had attended a school of theology but had merely memorized words and phrases, which meant little to him and nothing to those who heard his discourse. The school in which he had been trained followed the traditional course for ministers, devoting most of the time to dead languages and dead issues. He had given attention to polytheism, monotheism, and the doctrine of the Trinity. He had studied also the philosophical basis of the Caucasian dogma, the elements of that theology, and the schism by which fanatics made religion a football and multiplied wars only to moisten the soil of Europe with the blood of unoffending men.

This minister had given no attention to the religious background of the Negroes to whom he was trying to preach. He knew nothing of their spiritual endowment and their religious experience as influenced by their traditions and environment in which the religion of the Negro has developed and expressed itself. He did not seem to know anything about their present situation. These honest people, therefore, knew nothing additional when he had finished his discourse. As one communicant pointed out, their wants had not been supplied, and they wondered where they might go to hear a word which had some bearing upon the life which they had to live.

Not long ago when the author was in Virginia he inquired about a man who was once a popular preacher in that state. He is here, they said, but he is not preaching now. He went off to school, and when he came back the people could not understand what he was talking about. Then he began to find fault with the people because they would not come to church. He called them fogy, because they did not appreciate his new style of preaching and the things he talked about. The church went down to nothing, and he finally left it and took up farming.

In a rural community, then, a preacher of this type must fail unless he can organize separately members of the popular Methodist and Baptist churches who go into the ritualistic churches or establish certain "refined" Methodist or Baptist churches catering to the "talented tenth." For lack of adequate numbers, however, such churches often fail to develop sufficient force to do very much for themselves or for anybody else. On Sunday morning, then, their pastors have to talk to the benches. While these truncated churches go higher in their own atmosphere of self-satisfaction the mentally undeveloped are left to sink lower because of the lack of contact with the better trained. If the latter exercised a little more judgment, they would be able to influence these people for good by gradually introducing advanced ideas.

Because our "highly educated" people do not do this, large numbers of Negroes drift into churches led by the "uneducated" ministers who can scarcely read and write. These preachers do not know much of what is found in school books and can hardly make use of a library in working out a sermon; but they understand the people with whom they deal, and they make such use of the human laboratory that sometimes they become experts in solving vexing problems and meeting social needs. They would be much better preachers if they could have attended a school devoted to the development of the mind rather than to cramming it with extraneous matters which have no bearing on the task which lies before them. Unfortunately, however, very few of such schools of religion now exist.

For lack of intelligent guidance, then, the Negro church often fulfils a mission to the contrary of that for which it was established. Because the Negro church is such a free field and it is controlled largely by the Negroes themselves, it seems that practically all the incompetents and undesirables who have been barred from other walks of life by race prejudice and economic difficulties have rushed into the ministry for the exploitation of the people. Honest ministers who are trying to do their duty, then, find their task made difficult by these men who stoop to practically everything conceivable. Almost anybody of the lowest type may get into the Negro ministry. The Methodists claim that they have strict regulations to prevent this, but their net draws in proportionately as many undesirables as one finds among the Baptists.

As an evidence of the depths to which the institution has gone a resident of Cincinnati recently reported a case of its exploitation by a railroad man who lost his job and later all his earnings in a game in a den of vice in that city. To refinance himself he took an old black frock coat and a Bible and went into the heart of Tennessee, where he conducted at various points a series of distracted, protracted meetings which netted him two hundred and ninety-nine converts to the faith and four hundred dollars in cash. He was enabled thereby to return to the game in Cincinnati and he is still in the lead. Other such cases are frequently reported.

The large majority of Negro preachers of today, then, are doing nothing more than to keep up the medieval hell-fire scare which the whites have long since abandoned to emphasize the humanitarian trend in religion through systematized education. The young people of the Negro race could be held in the church by some such program, but the Negro's Christianity does not conceive of social uplift as a duty of the church; and consequently Negro children have not been adequately trained in religious matters to be equal to the social demands upon

them. Turning their back on medievalism, then, these un-
trained youth think nothing of taking up moonshining, gambling, and racketeering as occupations; and they find great joy
in smoking, drinking, and fornication as diversions. They cannot accept the old ideas, and they do not understand the new.

What the Negro church is, however, has been determined
largely by what the white man has taught the race by precept
and example. We must remember that the Negroes learned
their religion from the early white Methodists and Baptists
who evangelized the slaves and the poor whites when they
were barred from proselyting the aristocracy. The American
white people themselves taught Negroes to specialize unduly
in the "Praise the Lord," "Halleluiah" worship. In the West
Indies among the Anglicans and among the Latin people Negroes do not show such emotionalism. They are cold and conservative.

Some of the American whites, moreover, are just as far behind in this respect as are the Negroes who have had less opportunity to learn better. While in Miami, Florida, not long
ago the author found in two interracial "Holiness Churches"
that the following was a third or fourth white. The whites
joined whole-heartedly with the Negroes in their "holy roll-
ing" and some of them seemed to be "rollers not holy."

A few months ago in Huntington, West Virginia, where the
author was being entertained by friends, the party was disturbed throughout the evening by the most insane outbursts of
white worshippers in a "Church of God" across the street.
There they daily indulged in such whooping and screaming in
"unknown tongues" that the Negroes have had to report them
to the police as a nuisance. The author has made a careful
study of the Negro church, but he has never known Negroes to
do anything to surpass the performance of those heathen.

The American Negroes' ideas of morality, too, were borrowed from their owners. The Negroes could not be expected
to raise a higher standard than their aristocratic governing
class that teemed with sin and vice. This corrupt state of things
did not easily pass away. The Negroes have never seen any

striking examples among the whites to help them in matters of religion. Even during the colonial period the whites claimed that their ministers sent to the colonies by the Anglican Church, the progenitor of the Protestant Episcopal Church in America, were a degenerate class that exploited the people for money to waste it in racing horses and drinking liquor. Some of these ministers were known to have illicit relations with women and, therefore, winked at the sins of the officers of their churches, who sold their own offspring by slave women.

Although the author was born ten years after the Civil War the morals and religion of that regime continued even into his time. Many of the rich or well-to-do white men belonging to the churches in Buckingham County, Virginia, indulged in polygamy. They raised one family by a white woman and another by a colored or poor white woman. Both the owner of the largest slate quarry and the proprietor of the largest factory in that country lived in this fashion. One was an outstanding Episcopalian and the other a distinguished Catholic.

One day the foreman of the factory, a polygamous deacon of the local white Baptist Church, called the workmen together at noon for a short memorial service in honor of Parson Taylor, for almost half a century the pastor of the large white Baptist church in that section. The foreman made some remarks on the life of the distinguished minister, and then all sang "Shall We Meet Beyond the River?" But "to save his life" the author could not restrain himself from wondering all that time whether the foreman's white wife or colored paramour would greet him on the other side, and what a conflict there would be if they happened to get into an old-fashioned hair-pulling. In spite of his libertine connections, however, this foreman believed that he was a Christian, and when he died his eulogist commended his soul to God.

Some years later when the author was serving his six years' apprenticeship in the West Virginia coal mines he found at Nutallburg a very faithful vestryman of the white Episcopal Church at that point. He was one of the most devout from the point of view of his co-workers. Yet, privately, this man boasted of having participated in that most brutal lynching of the four Negroes who thus met their doom at the hands of an angry mob in Clifton Forge, Virginia, in 1892.

It is very clear, then, that if Negroes got their conception of religion from slaveholders, libertines, and murderers, there may be something wrong about it, and it would not hurt to investigate it. It has been said that the Negroes do not connect morals with religion. The historian would like to know what race or nation does such a thing. Certainly the whites with whom the Negroes have come into contact have not done so.

CHAPTER VIII

PROFESSIONAL EDUCATION
DISCOURAGED

In the training for professions other than the ministry and teaching the Negro has not had full sway. Any extensive comment on professional education by the Negro, then, must be mainly negative. We have not had sufficient professional schools upon which we can base an estimate of what the Negro educator can do in this sphere. If mistakes have been made in miseducating the Negro professionally it must be charged not so much to the account of the Negroes themselves as to that of their friends who have performed this task. We are dealing here, then, mainly with information obtained from the study of Negroes who have been professionally trained by whites in their own schools and in mixed institutions.

The largest numbers of Negroes in professions other than the ministry or education are physicians, dentists, pharmacists, lawyers and actors. The numbers in these and other lines have not adequately increased because of the economic status of the Negroes and probably because of a false conception of the role of the professional man in the community and its relation to him. The people whom the Negro professional men have volunteered to serve have not always given them sufficient support to develop that standing and solidarity which will make their position professional and influential. Most whites in contact with Negroes, always the teachers of their brethren in black, both by precept and practice, have treated the professions as aristocratic spheres to which Negroes should not aspire. We have had, then, a much smaller number than those who under different circumstances would have dared to cross the line; and those that did so were starved out by the whites who would not treat them as a professional class. This made it impracticable for Negroes to employ them in spheres in which they could not function efficiently. For example, because of a law that a man could not be admitted to the bar in Delaware without practicing a year under some lawyer in the state (and no white lawyer would grant a Negro such an opportunity until a few years ago) it was only recently that a Negro was admitted there.

Negroes, then, learned from their oppressors to say to their children that there were certain spheres into which they should not go because they would have no chance therein for development. In a number of places young men were discouraged and frightened away from certain professions by the poor showing made by those trying to function in them. Few had the courage to face this ordeal; and some professional schools in institutions for Negroes were closed about thirty or forty years ago, partly on this account.

This was especially true of the law schools, closed during the wave of legislation against the Negro, at the very time the largest possible number of Negroes needed to know the law for the protection of their civil and political rights. In other words, the thing which the patient needed most to pass the crisis was taken from him that he might more easily die. This one act among many others is an outstanding monument to the stupidity or malevolence of those in charge of Negro schools, and it serves as a striking demonstration of the mis-education of the race.

Almost any observer remembers distinctly the hard trials of the Negro lawyers. A striking example of their difficulties was supplied by the case of the first to be permanently established in Huntington, West Virginia. The author had entrusted to him the matter of correcting an error in the transfer of some property purchased from one of the most popular white attorneys in the state. For six months this simple transaction was delayed, and the Negro lawyer could not induce the white attorney to act. The author finally went to the office himself to complain of the delay. The white attorney frankly declared that he had not taken up the matter because he did not care to treat with a Negro attorney; but he would deal with the author, who happened to be at that time the teacher of a Negro school, and was, therefore, in his place.

At one time the Negroes in medicine and correlated fields were regarded in the same light. They had difficulty in making their own people believe that they could cure a complaint, fill a tooth, or compound a prescription. The whites said that they could not do it; and, of course, if the whites said so, it was true, so far as most Negroes were concerned. In those fields, however, actual demonstrations to the contrary have convinced a sufficient number of both Negroes and whites that such an attitude toward these classes is false, but there are many Negroes who still follow those early teachings, especially the "highly educated" who in school have been given the "scientific" reasons for it. It is a most remarkable process that while in one department of a university a Negro may be studying for a profession, in another department of the same university he is being shown how the Negro professional man cannot succeed. Some of the "highly educated," then, give their practice to those who are often inferior to the Negroes whom they thus pass by. Although there has been an increase in these particular spheres, however, the professions among Negroes, with the exception of teaching and preaching, are still undermanned.

In the same way the Negro was once discouraged and dissuaded from taking up designing, drafting, architecture, engineering and chemistry. The whites, they were told, will not employ you and your people cannot provide such opportunities. The thought of pioneering or of developing the Negro to the extent that he might figure in this sphere did not dawn on those monitors of the Negroes preparing for their life's work. This tradition is still a heavy load in Negro education, and it forces many Negroes out of spheres in which they might function into those for which they may not have any aptitude.

In music, dramatics and correlated arts, too, the Negro has been unfortunately misled. Because the Negro is gifted as a

singer and can render more successfully than others the music
of his own people, he has been told that he does not need
training. Scores of those who have undertaken to function in
this sphere without adequate education, then, have developed
only to a certain point beyond which they have not had ability
to go. We cannot easily estimate how popular Negro musi-
cians and their music might have become had they been taught
to the contrary.

Of these, several instances may be cited. A distinguished
man, talking recently as a member of a large Episcopal church,
which maintains a Negro mission, mentioned his objection to
the budget of fifteen hundred dollars a year for music for these
segregated communicants. Inasmuch as the Negroes were naturally gifted in music he did not believe that any expensive
training or direction was required. The small number of Negro
colleges and universities which undertake the training of the
Negro in music is further evidence of the belief that the Negro
is all but perfect in this field and should direct his attention to
the traditional curricula.

The same misunderstanding with respect to the Negro in
dramatics is also evident. We have long had the belief that the
Negro is a natural actor who does not require any stimulus for
further development. In this assertion is the idea that because
the Negro is good at dancing, joking, minstrelsy and the like
he is "in his place" when "cutting a shine" and does not need
to be trained to function in the higher sphere of dramatics.
Thus misled, large numbers of Negroes ambitious for the stage
have not bloomed forth into great possibilities. Too many of
them have finally ended with roles in questionable cafés, caba-
rets, and night clubs of America and Europe; and instead of
increasing the prestige of the Negro they have brought the race
into disgrace.

We scarcely realize what a poor showing we make in dramatics in spite of our natural aptitude in this sphere. Only
about a half dozen Negro actors have achieved greatness, but
we have more actors and showmen than any other profession-
als except teachers and ministers. Where are these thousands
of men and women in the histrionic sphere? What do we hear

of them? What have they achieved? Their record shows that only a few measure up to the standard of the modern stage. Most of these would-be artists have no preparation for the tasks undertaken.

A careful study of the Negro in dramatics shows that only those who have actually taken the time to train themselves as they should be have finally endured. Their salvation has been to realize that adequate training is the surest way to attain artistic maturity. And those few who have thus understood the situation clearly demonstrate our ineptitude in the failure to educate the Negroes along the lines in which they could have admirably succeeded. Some of our schools have for some time undertaken this work as imitators of institutions dealing with persons otherwise circumstanced. Desirable results, therefore, have not followed, and the Negro on the stage is still mainly the product of the trial and error method.

Several other reasons may be given for the failure of a larger number of Negro actors to reach a higher level. In the first place, they have been recognized by the white man only in purely plantation comedy and minstrelsy, and because of the large number entering the field it has failed to offer a bright future for many of such aspirants. Repeatedly told by the white man that he could not function as an actor in a different sphere, the American Negro has all but ceased to attempt anything else. The successful career of Ira Aldridge[1] in Shakespeare was forgotten until recently recalled by the dramatic success of Paul Robeson in Othello. The large majority of Negroes have settled down, then, to contentment as ordinary clowns and comedians. They have not had the courage or they have not learned how to break over the unnatural barriers and occupy higher ground.

The Negro author is no exception to the traditional rule. He writes, but the white man is supposed to know more about everything than the Negro. So who wants a book written by a Negro about one? As a rule, not even a Negro himself, for if he is really "educated," he must show that he has the appreciation for the best in literature. The Negro author, then, can neither find a publisher nor a reader; and his story remains untold.

The Negro editors and reporters were once treated the same way, but thanks to the uneducated printers who founded most of our newspapers which have succeeded, these men of vision have made it possible for the "educated" Negroes to make a living in this sphere in proportion as they recover from their education and learn to deal with the Negro as he is and where he is.

CHAPTER IX

POLITICAL EDUCATION NEGLECTED

Some time ago when Congressman Oscar De Priest[1] was distributing by thousands copies of the Constitution of the United States certain wiseacres were disposed to make fun of it. What purpose would such an act serve? These critics, however, probably did not know that thousands and thousands of Negro children in this country are not permitted to use school books in which are printed the Declaration of Independence or the Constitution of the United States. Thomas Jefferson and James Madison are mentioned in their history as figures in politics rather than as expounders of liberty and freedom. These youths are not permitted to learn that Jefferson believed that government should derive its power from the consent of the governed.

Not long ago a measure was introduced in a certain State Legislature to have the Constitution of the United States thus printed in school histories, but when the bill was about to pass it was killed by some one who made the point that it would never do to have Negroes study the Constitution of the United States. If the Negroes were granted the opportunity to peruse this document, they might learn to contend for the rights therein guaranteed; and no Negro teacher who gives attention to such matters of the government is tolerated in those backward districts. The teaching of government or the lack of such instruction, then, must be made to conform to the policy of "keeping the Negro in his place."

In like manner, the teaching of history in the Negro area has had its political significance. Starting out after the Civil War, the opponents of freedom and social justice decided to work out a program which would enslave the Negroes' mind inasmuch as the freedom of body had to be conceded. It was well understood that if by teaching of history the white man could be further assured of his superiority and the Negro could be made to feel that he had always been a failure and that the subjection of his will to some other race is necessary the freedman, then, would still be a slave. If you can control a man's thinking you do not have to worry about his action. When you determine what a man shall think you do not have to concern yourself about what he will do. If you make a man feel that he is inferior, you do not have to compel him to accept an inferior status, for he will seek it himself. If you make a man think that he is justly an outcast, you do not have to order him to the back door. He will go without being told; and if there is no back door, his very nature will demand one.

This program, so popular immediately after the Civil War, was not new, but after this upheaval, its execution received a new stimulus. Histories written elsewhere for the former slave area were discarded, and new treatments of local and national history in conformity with the recrudescent propaganda were produced to give whites and blacks the biased point of view of the development of the nation and the relations of the races. Special treatments of the Reconstruction period were produced in apparently scientific form by propagandists who went into the first graduate schools of the East to learn modern historiography about half a century ago. Having the stamp of science, the thought of these polemics was accepted in all seats of learning. These rewriters of history fearlessly contended that slavery was a benevolent institution; the masters loved their slaves and treated them humanely; the abolitionists meddled with the institution which the masters eventually would have modified; the Civil War brought about by "fanatics" like William Lloyd Garrison and John Brown[2] was unnecessary; it was a mistake to make the Negro a citizen, for he merely became worse off by incurring the displeasure of the master class that will never tolerate him as an equal; and the Negro must live in this country in a state of recognized inferiority.

Some of these theories may seem foolish, but historians even in the North have been won to this point of view. They ignore the recent works of Miss Elizabeth Donnan, Mrs. H. T. Catterall, and Dr. Frederic Bancroft,[3] who have spent years investigating slavery and slave-trading. These are scientific productions with the stamp of the best scholarship in America, treatises produced from such genuine documents as the court records of the slaveholding section itself, and these authors have rendered the public a valuable service in removing the whitewash which pseudo-historians have been giving to slavery and slaveholders for more than a century.

In the preparation of Negroes, many of whom teach in the South, these biased Northern historians even convert them to such a faith. A few years ago the author happened to listen to a conversation of Negro lawyers in one of our Southern cities, in which they unanimously conceded practically every contention set forth in this program of propaganda. They denounced, therefore, all reconstructionists who advocated equality and justice for all. These Negroes had the biased point of view of the rewriters like Claude Bowers and had never been directed to the real history of that drama as set forth by A. A. Taylor, Francis B. Simkins and Robert H. Woody of the new Southern school of thought.[4] These Negro critics were especially hard on Negroes of our day who engage in agitation for actual democracy. Negroes themselves in certain parts join with the whites, then, in keeping out of the schools teachers who may be bold enough to teach the truth as it is. They usually say the races here are getting along amicably now, and we do not want these peaceful relations disturbed by the teaching of new political thought.

What they mean to say with respect to the peaceful relation of the races, then, is that the Negroes have been terrorized to the extent that they are afraid even to discuss political matters publicly. There must be no exposition of the principles of government in the schools, and this must not be done in public among Negroes with a view to stimulating political activity. Negroes engaged in other spheres in such communities finally come to the point of accepting silence on these matters as a fixed policy. Knowing that action to the contrary means mob rule which may destroy the peace and property of the community, they constitute themselves a sort of a vigilant committee to direct their fellows accordingly.

A few years ago a rather youthful looking high school principal in one of the large cities was unceremoniously dismissed because he said jocosely to the president of the board of education, in reply to his remark about his youthful bearing, "I am old enough to vote." "Horrors!" said the infuriated official. "Put him out. We brought him here to teach these Negroes how to work, and here he is thinking about voting." A few prominent Negroes of the place muttered a little, but they did nothing effective to correct this injustice.

In certain parts, therefore, the Negroes under such terrorism have ceased to think of political matters as their sphere. Where such things come into the teaching in more advanced work they are presented as matters of concern to a particular element rather than as functions in which all citizens may participate. The result is that Negroes grow up without knowledge of political matters which should concern all elements. To prevent the Negroes from learning too much about these things the whites in the schools are sometimes neglected also, but the latter have the opportunity to learn by contact, close observation, and actual participation in the affairs of government.

Negroes in certain parts, then, have all but abandoned voting even at points where it might be allowed. In some cases not as many as two thousand Negroes vote in a whole state. By special legislation providing for literacy tests and the payment of taxes their number of voters has been reduced to a negligible quantity, and the few who can thus function do not do so because they are often counted out when they have the deciding vote.

The tests established for the restriction of suffrage were not intended to stimulate political education but to eliminate the Negro vote by subterfuge. Negroes presenting themselves for registration are asked to do the all but impossible thing of ex-pounding parts of the Constitution which have baffled high courts; but whites are asked simple questions which almost any illiterate man can answer. In this way the Negroes, how-ever intelligent, are turned down; and all ignorant whites are permitted to vote. These laws, then, have retarded rather than stimulated the political education of both races. Such knowl-edge is apparently useless for Negroes and unnecessary for the whites, for the Negroes do not immediately profit by having it and the whites may function as citizens without it.

The effect of such a one-sided system is decidedly bad. One does not realize it until he talks with men and women of these districts, who because of the denial of these privileges have lost interest in political matters. A book agent working in the plantation area of Mississippi tested the knowledge of Ne-groes of these matters by asking them questions about the local and State government. He discovered that they knew practically nothing in this sphere. It was difficult to find any who knew who was president of the United States. One meets teachers, physicians, and ministers who do not know the ordi-nary operations of courts, the functions of the counsel, jury or judge, unless such knowledge has come by the bitter experi-ence of having been imposed upon by some tribunal of injus-tice. Some of the "educated" Negroes do not pay attention to such important matters as the assessment of property and the collection of taxes, and they do not inform themselves as to how these things are worked out. An influential Negro in the South, then, is one who has nothing to do or say about politics and advises others to follow the same course.

The elimination of the Negro from politics, then, has been most unfortunate. The whites may have profited thereby tem-porarily, but they showed very little foresight. How the whites can expect to make of the Negroes better citizens by leading them to think that they should have no part in the government of this country is a mystery. To keep a man above vagabond-age and crime he needs among other things the stimulus of pa-triotism, but how can a man be patriotic when the effect of his education is to the contrary?

What little chance the Negro has to learn by participation in politics in most parts of the South is unfortunately restricted now to corruption. The usual stir about electing delegates to the National Republican Convention from the Southern States and the customary combat the Negroes have with Lily-white corruptionists are about all the political matters which claim their attention in the Lower South. Neither the white nor the black faction, as a rule, makes any effort to restore suffrage to Negroes. The objective is merely the control of delegates and Federal patronage for the financial considerations involved. To do this they resort to numerous contests culminating in closing hotels and bolting doors for secret meetings. Since this is the only activity in which Negroes can participate they have learned to look upon it as honorable. Large numbers of Negroes become excited over the contest and give much publicity to it on the rostrum and in the press as a matter of great importance. The methods of these corruptionists of both races, however, should be condemned as a disgrace to the state and nation.

Instead of doing something to get rid of this ilk, however, we find the "highly educated" Negroes trying to plunge also into the mire. One of the most discouraging aspects in Negro life recently observed was that of a presidential campaign. Prominent Negroes connected with three of our leading institutions of learning temporarily abandoned their work to round up Negro votes for one of the candidates. The objective, of course, was to control the few ordinary jobs which are allotted to Negro politicians for their campaign services. When the successful candidate had been inaugurated, however, he carefully ignored them in the make-up of the personnel of his administration and treated Negroes in general with contempt. When you think of the fact that the Negroes who are being thus used are supposedly the most reputable Negro leaders and our most highly educated men you have to wonder whether the Negro has made any progress since Emancipation. The only consolation one can get out of it is that they may not represent the whole race.

In the North the Negroes have a better chance to acquire

knowledge of political matters of the simple kind, but the bosses do not think it is advisable to enlighten them thoroughly. Negroes in parts are employed in campaigns, but they are not supposed to discuss such issues of the day as free trade, tariff for protection, the World Court, and the League of Nations. These Negro workers are supposed to tell their people how one politician seeking office has appointed more Negro messengers or charwomen in the service than the other or how the grandfather of the candidate stood with Lincoln and Grant through their ordeal and thus brought the race into its own. Another important task of these Negroes thus employed is also to abuse the opposing party, showing how hostile it has been to the Negro while the highly favorable party was doing so much for the race.

The course of these bosses has been interesting. At first the white man used the Negro leader by giving him a drink occasionally. The next step was to give him sufficient money to set up drinks in the name of the white candidate. When drinking at the expense of the candidate became too common the politicians fell back on the distribution of funds in small amounts. When this finally proved to be insufficient, however, the politicians had to go a bit further and provide Jim Crow jobs in certain backrooms with the understanding that the functions of the so-called office would be merely nominal and the incumbents would have no close contact with white people. In this stage the Negroes find themselves today.

The undesirable aspect of the affair is that the Negro in spite of the changes from one method of approach to that of another is never brought into the inner circle of the party with which he is affiliated. He is always kept on the outside and is used as a means to an end. To obtain the meager consideration which he receives the Negro must work clandestinely through the back door. It has been unnecessary for the white man to change this procedure, for until recent years he has generally found it possible to satisfy the majority of Negroes with the few political positions earmarked as "Negro jobs" and to crush those who clamor for more recognition.

It is unfortunate, too, that such a large number of Negroes

do not know any better than to stake their whole fortune on politics. History does not show that any race, especially a minority group, has ever solved an important problem by relying altogether on one thing, certainly not by parking its political strength on one side of the fence because of empty promises. There are Negroes who know better, but such thinkers are kept in the background by the traducers of the race to prevent the enlightenment of the masses. The misleading politicians are the only persons through whom the traducers act with respect to the Negro, and there are always a sufficient number of mentally undeveloped voters who will supply them a large following.

Even the few Negroes who are elected to office are often similarly uniformed and show a lack of vision. They have given little attention to the weighty problems of the nation; and in the legislative bodies to which they are elected, they restrict themselves as a rule to matters of special concern to the Negroes themselves, such as lynching, segregation and disfranchisement, which they have well learned by experience. This indicates a step backwards, for the Negroes who sat in Congress and in the State Legislatures during the Reconstruction worked for the enactment of measures of concern to all elements of the population regardless of color. Historians have not yet forgot what those Negro statesmen did in advocating public education, internal improvements, labor arbitration, the tariff, and the merchant marine.

CHAPTER X

THE LOSS OF VISION

History shows, then, that as a result of these unusual forces in the education of the Negro he easily learns to follow the line of least resistance rather than battle against odds for what real history has shown to be the right course. A mind that remains in the present atmosphere never undergoes sufficient development to experience what is commonly known as thinking. No Negro thus submerged in the ghetto, then, will have a clear conception of the present status of the race or sufficient foresight to plan for the future; and he drifts so far toward compromise that he loses moral courage. The education of the Negro, then, becomes a perfect device for control from without. Those who purposely promote it have every reason to rejoice, and Negroes themselves exultingly champion the cause of the oppressor.

A comparison of the record of the spokesmen of the race today with that of those of the eighteenth century shows a moral surrender. During the prolonged struggle between the French and English in America the Negroes held the balance of power at several strategic points and used it accordingly; today the Negro finds himself inconsequential because he can be parked on one side of the fence. The same balance of power was evident also during the American Revolution when Negro soldiers insisted on serving side by side with others; today many Negroes are content as menials in the army. At that time Negroes preached to mixed congregations; today we find Negroes busy separating them. The eighteenth-century Negro resented any such thing as social distinctions; today Negroes are saying that they do not want social equality. Negroes of that

epoch said with the ancient poet, "I am a man and deem nothing that relates to man a matter of indifference to me"; today,
however, the average Negro says, "Now, I am a colored man,
and you white folks must settle that matter among yourselves."

At a still later date the American Negro showed more courage than he does today with all of his so-called enlightenment.
When the free Negroes were advised a hundred years ago to
go to Africa they replied that they would never separate themselves from the slave population of this country as they were
brethren by the "ties of consanguinity, of suffering, and of
wrong." Today, however, the Negro in the North turns up his
nose at the crude migrant from the South who brings to the
North the race problem but along with it more thrift and actual progress than the Northern Negro ever dreamed of.

When, again in 1816,[1] free Negroes like Richard Allen,
James Forten, and Robert Purvis, were referred to as a foreign
element whose social status might not be secure in this country, instead of permitting the colonizationists to shove them
aside as criminals to be deported to a distant shore, they replied in no uncertain terms that this soil in America which
gave them birth is their only true home. "Here their fathers
fought, bled, and died for this country and here they intended
to stay." Today when such things come up you find Negroes
appearing upon the scene to see how much pay they can obtain to assist in the proposed undoing of the race.

Further emphasizing this thought of resistance a few years
later, Nathaniel Paul, a Baptist preacher of Albany, informed
the colonizationists that the free Negroes would not permit
their traducers to formulate a program for the race. You may
go ahead with your plan to deport this element in order to
make slavery secure, he warned; but the free Negroes will
never emigrate to Africa. "We shall stay here and fight until
the foul monster is crushed. Slavery must go."

"Did I believe it would always continue," said he, "and that
man to the end of time would be permitted with impunity to
usurp the same undue authority over his fellow, I would dis-
avow any allegiance or obligation I was under to my fellow
creatures, or any submission that I owed to the laws of my

country! I would deny the superintending power of divine Providence in the affairs of this life; I would ridicule the religion of the Savior of the world, and treat as the worst of men the ministers of the everlasting gospel; I would consider my Bible as a book of false and delusive fables, and commit it to the flames; nay, I would still go farther; I would at once confess myself an atheist, and deny the existence of a holy God."

And these Negroes of a century ago stood their ground and fought the pro-slavery deportationists to a standstill, for with the exception of a few pioneers the emigrants to Liberia were largely slaves manumitted on the condition that they would settle in Africa. These freedmen, then, could have no ideals but those of the slaveholding section from which they were sent. They established, therefore, a slavocracy in Liberia. If Liberia has failed, then, it is no evidence of the failure of the Negro in government. It is merely evidence of the failure of slavery.

The Negroes attacking Jim-Crowism almost a century ago fearlessly questioned the constitutionality of such a provision. Speaking through Charles Lenox Remond[2] of that day, they said, "There is a distinction between social and civil rights. We all claim the privilege of selecting our society and associations, but, in civil rights, one man has not the prerogative to define rights for another. These [race] distinctions react in all their wickedness—to say nothing of their concocted and systematized odiousness and absurdity—upon those who are illiberal and mean enough to practice them."

In our day, however, we find some "highly educated" Negroes approving such Jim-Crowism. For example, not many years ago an outstanding Baptist preacher, dabbling in politics in West Virginia, suggested to the whites that they enact a Jim Crow car law in that State, and we had difficulty in crushing that sentiment. A few years thereafter the author heard one of our bishops say that we should not object to such separation, for we want to be by ourselves. When this distinguished churchman died the traducers of the Negro lauded him to the skies; and thoughtless members of the race, thinking that he deserved it, joined in the loud acclaim.

In this way the large majority of "educated" Negroes in the United States have accepted segregation and have become its fearless champions. Their filled but undeveloped minds do not enable them to understand that, although an opiate furnishes temporary relief, it does not remove the cause of the pain. In this case we have yielded on principle to satisfy the mob, but have not yet found an ultimate solution of the problem at hand. In our so-called democracy we are accustomed to give the majority what they want rather than educate them to understand what is best for them. We do not show the Negro how to overcome segregation, but we teach him how to accept it as final and just.

Numerous results from this policy may be cited. The white laboring man refuses to work with Negroes because of the false tradition that the Negro is an inferior, and at the same time the Negro for the same reason becomes content with menial service and drudgery. The politician excludes the Negro from the councils of his party and from the government because he has been taught that such is necessary to maintain the supremacy of his race; the Negro, trained in the same school of thought, accepts this as final and contends for such meager consideration as the bosses may begrudgingly grant him. An irate resident in an exclusive district protests against an invasion by Negroes because he has learned that these poverty-stricken people are carriers of disease and agents of crime; the Negroes, believing that such is the truth, remain content in the ghetto. The irrational parent forces the separation of the races in some schools because his child must occupy a seat next to a pupil of "tainted" African blood; the educated Negro accepts this as inevitable and welcomes the makeshift for his people. Children of Negroes are excluded from the playgrounds because of the assertion that they will contaminate those of the whites; the Negroes yielding, settle down to a policy of having their children grow up in neglected fashion in the most undesirable part of the city. The Negro is forced to ride in a Jim Crow car to stamp upon him more easily the badge of his "inferiority"; the "educated Negro" accepts it as settled and abandons the fight against this social proscription.

And thus goes segregation which is the most far-reaching development in the history of the Negro since the enslavement of the race. In fact, it is a sequel of slavery. It has been made possible by our system of mis-educating innocent people who did not know what was happening. It is so subtle that men have participated in promoting it without knowing what they were doing.

There are a few defenders of segregation who are doubtless sincere. Although nominally free they have never been sufficiently enlightened to see the matter other than as slaves. One can cite cases of Negroes who opposed emancipation and denounced the abolitionists. A few who became free reenslaved themselves. A still larger number made no effort to become free because they did not want to disconnect themselves from their masters, and their kind still object to full freedom.

Ever since the Civil War when Negroes were first given a chance to participate in the management of their affairs they have been inconsistent and compromising. They have tried to gain one thing on one day by insisting on equality for all, while at the same time endeavoring to gain another point the next day by segregation. At one moment Negroes fight for the principle of democracy, and at the very next moment they barter it away for some temporary advantage. You cannot have a thing and dispose of it at the same time.

For example, the Negro political leaders of the Reconstruction period clamored for suffrage and the right of holding office, serving in the militia, and sitting on the jury; but few of them wanted white and colored children to attend the same school. When expressing themselves on education most of them took the position of segregationists; and Charles Sumner[3] in his fight for the civil rights of the Negro had to eliminate mixed schools from his program not only because many whites objected but also because the Negroes themselves did not seem to want them. All of these leaders might not have been looking for jobs in those days; but as nominal freemen, who were still slaves, they did not feel comfortable in the presence of their former masters.

These timorous men were very much like some Negroes who

were employed near the author's home in Virginia by a Northern farmer, who had moved into the State after the Civil War. When breakfast time came the first morning he called them in to eat at the table with his family. These actual slaves, however, immediately lost their appetite. One finally called the employer aside and settled the matter in another way. He said:

"Now boss, you ain't used to de rules ob dis country. We just can't sit at de table wid wite folks. We been use ter eating a cake er bread out yonder 'tween de plow handles. Les us go out dar."

The system, therefore, has extended from one thing to another until the Negroes today find themselves hedged in by the color bar almost every way they turn; and, set off by themselves, the Negroes cannot learn from the example of others with whom they might come into contact. In the ghetto, too, they are not permitted to construct and carry out a program of their own. These segregating institutions interfere with the development of self-help among Negroes, for often Negroes fail to raise money to establish institutions which they might control, but they readily contribute large sums for institutions which segregate persons of African blood.

Denied participation in the higher things of life, the "educated" Negro himself joins, too, with ill-designing persons to handicap his people by systematized exploitation. Feeling that the case of the Negro is hopeless, the "educated" Negro decides upon the course of personally profiting by whatever he can do in using these people as a means to an end. He grins in their faces while "extracting money" from them, but his heart shows no fond attachment to their despised cause. With a little larger income than they receive he can make himself somewhat comfortable in the ghetto; and he forgets those who have no way of escape.

Some of this "educated" class join with unprincipled real estate men in keeping Negroes out of desirable parts of the city and confining them to unsanitary sections. Such persons help the profiteer to collect from Negroes thus cornered a larger rental than that exacted from whites for the same property. In similar fashion a Negro minister sometimes goes into a community where the races are moving along amicably together in their churches and rents a shack or an old empty store to start a separate church for "our people," not to supply any practical need but to exploit those who have never learned to think. Professional men, too, walking in their footsteps, impose also upon the poor innocent Negroes who do not know when they are being treated properly and when they are not, but high fees may be obtained from them inasmuch as they cannot always go to others for service.

Settling in a community with mixed schools, the educated Negro often advocates their separation that his daughter may secure a position in the system. The Negro politician is accustomed to corner the Negro vote, by opening a separate office from which he may bargain with the chieftains of the machine for the highest price available. When paid off by some position, which is not very lofty, this office holder accepts such employment with the understanding that he will be set off by himself as if he were destructive of the rest of mankind.

In the present crisis, however, the "highly educated" Negroes find very little to exploit, and in their untoward condition they have no program of finding a way out. They see numerous instances of Negroes losing their jobs in white establishments. In fact, these things occur daily. Janitors who have been giving satisfaction are abruptly told that they will no longer be needed. Negro waiters in hotels are being informed that their places will go to white workers. Negro truck drivers are ordered to step down and let the needy of the other race go up. We hear so much of this that we wonder what the outcome will be.

In this readjustment, of course, when there are fewer opportunities left for those who cannot or do not have the opportunity to operate machines the Negroes will naturally be turned out of their positions by their employers who think first of their own race. In the ultimate passing of the depression,[4] however, Negroes will not be much better off when some of the whites now displacing them will rise to higher levels. In the economic order of tomorrow there will be little use for the factotum or scullion. Man will not need such personal attention when he can buy a machine to serve him more efficiently. The menial Negroes, the aggregate of parasites whom the "highly educated" Negro has exploited, will not be needed on tomorrow. What, then, will become of "our highly educated" Negroes who have no initiative?

We have appealed to the talented tenth for a remedy, but they have nothing to offer. Their minds have never functioned in this all-important sphere. The "educated" Negro shows no evidence of vision. He should see a new picture. The Negroes are facing the alternative of rising in the sphere of production to supply their proportion of the manufacturers and merchants or of going down to the graves of paupers. The Negro must now do for himself or die out as the world undergoes readjustment. If the whites are to continue for some time in doing drudgery to the exclusion of Negroes, the latter must find another way out. Nothing forces this upon one more dramatically than when he learns that white women in Montgomery, Alabama, are coming to the back door of Negro homes asking for their washing. If the whites have reached this extremity, and they must be taken care of first, what will be left for the Negroes?

At this moment, then, the Negroes must begin to do the very thing which they have been taught that they cannot do. They still have some money, and they have needs to supply. They must begin immediately to pool their earnings and organize industries to participate in supplying social and economic demands. If the Negroes are to remain forever removed from the producing atmosphere, and the present discrimination continues, there will be nothing left for them to do.

There is no reason for lack of confidence because of the recent failure of Negro enterprises, although the "highly educated" Negroes assert the contrary. This lack of confidence is the cause of the failure of these enterprises. If the Negroes had manifested enough confidence in them and had properly supported them, they would have been strong enough to stand the test in the crisis. Negro banks, as a rule, have failed because the people, taught that their own pioneers in business cannot function in this sphere, withdrew their deposits. An individual cannot live after you extract the blood from his veins. The strongest bank in the United States will last only so long as the people will have sufficient confidence in it to keep their money there. In fact, the confidence of the people is worth more than money.

The lack of confidence of the Negro in himself and in his possibilities is what has kept him down. His mis-education has been a perfect success in this respect. Yet it is not necessary for the Negro to have more confidence in his own workers than in others. If the Negro would be as fair to his own as he has been to others, this would be all that is necessary to give him a new lease on life and start the trend upward.

Here we find that the Negro has failed to recover from his slavish habit of berating his own and worshipping others as perfect beings. No progress has been made in this respect because the more "education" the Negro gets the worse off he is. He has just had so much longer to learn to decry and despise himself. The race looking to this educated class for a solution of its problems does not find any remedy; and, on the contrary, sees itself further and further away from those things to which it has aspired. By forgetting the schoolroom for the time being and relying upon an awakening of the masses through adult education we can do much to give the Negro a new point of view with respect to economic enterprise and group cooperation. The average Negro has not been sufficiently mis-educated to become hopeless.

Our minds must become sufficiently developed to use segregation to kill segregation, and thus bring to pass that ancient and yet modern prophecy, "The wrath of man shall praise thee." If the Negro in the ghetto must eternally be fed by the hand that pushes him into the ghetto, he will never become strong enough to get out of the ghetto. This assumption of Negro leadership in the ghetto, then, must not be confined to matters of religion, education, and social uplift; it must deal with such fundamental forces in life as make these things possible. If the Negro area, however, is to continue as a district supported wholly from without, the inept dwellers therein will merit and will receive only the contempt of those who may occasionally catch glimpses of them in their plight.

As Frederick Douglass said in 1852, "It is vain that we talk of being men, if we do not the work of men. We must become valuable to society in other departments of industry than those servile ones from which we are rapidly being excluded. We must show that we can do as well as they. When we can build as well as live in houses; when we can make as well as wear shoes; when we can produce as well as consume wheat, corn and rye—then we shall become valuable to society.

"Society," continued Douglass, "is a hard-hearted affair. With it the helpless may expect no higher dignity than that of paupers. The individual must lay society under obligation to him or society will honor him only as a stranger and so-journer."

CHAPTER XI

THE NEED FOR SERVICE
RATHER THAN LEADERSHIP

In this untoward situation the Negro finds himself at the close of the third generation from Emancipation. He has been educated in the sense that persons directed a certain way are more easily controlled, or as Ovid remarked, "In time the bull is brought to bear the yoke." The Negro in this state continues as a child. He is restricted in his sphere to small things, and with these he becomes satisfied. His ambition does not rise any higher than to plunge into the competition with his fellows for these trifles. At the same time those who have given the race such false ideals are busy in the higher spheres from which Negroes by their mis-education and racial guidance have been disbarred.

Examples of this failure of the mis-educated Negro to have high ideals may be cited. The author has known numerous cases of Negro lawyers, physicians and business men who, while attending local Sunday schools, churches, and lodges, have fallen out about trifles like a resolution or the chairmanship of a committee, which so embittered them as to make themselves enemies for life and stumbling blocks preventing any such thing as organization or community cooperation.

It is a common occurrence to see a Negro well situated as a minister or teacher aspiring to a political appointment which temporarily pays little more than what he is receiving and offers no distinction except that of being earmarked as a Jim Crow job set aside for some Negro who has served well the purposes of the bosses as a ward-heeler in a campaign.

Negroes who have begun promising business enterprises sometimes abandon them temporarily for the same sort of empty
honor. In this way they have been known to hamper their business by incurring the displeasure of ambitious politicians who
might otherwise patronize them.

Negroes of this point of view have developed in that part of
the country where it is thought that the most distinguished
persons in the community are those who hold and exploit the
local offices or those who are further honored with positions
in the state and nation. While this may apply in the case of
their oppressors the few positions allotted the Negroes are
magnified beyond all reasonable bounds. This comes as a natural result, however, for the "education" of the Negro requires
it. The ambitious mis-educated Negro in the struggle for the
little things allotted by others prevents any achievement of the
people in matters more constructive. Potentially the colored
people are strong although they are actually weak.

This much-ado-about-nothing renders impossible cooperation, the most essential thing in the development of a people.
The ambitious of this class do more to keep the race in a state
of turmoil and to prevent it from serious community effort
than all the other elements combined. The one has a job that
the other wants; or the one is a leader of a successful faction,
and the other is struggling to supplant him. Everything in the
community, then, must yield ground to this puerile contest.

In one city of a few thousand Negroes there is no chance for
community cooperation because of the antagonism of the
Methodist and Baptist preachers in charge of the two largest
churches. The one is determined to dictate the appointment of
the teaching corps and the social welfare workers; the other is
persistently struggling to undo everything accomplished by his
opponent. The one is up today, and the other in ascendency tomorrow. Several efforts have been made to start business enterprises there, but none has succeeded because one faction
tears down what the other builds up.

In another city the cleavage is along political lines. Preachers are there, but a lawyer and a dentist plunging into politics
have dispossessed the clergy of the stage. The leader of one

faction is so bitterly opposed to the other that he even warns strangers against going to the home of his adversary. To present a sane proposition to the community through one of these leaders means local warfare rather than an effort to work together for the common good. Consequently, although there are thousands of Negroes living together in one quarter they have no business enterprises of worth. The selfish struggle for personal aggrandizement, which has not yet brought either faction more than an appointment on the police force or a clerkship in one of the city offices, thus blocks the social and economic progress of thousands of unoffending people.

In another state the ambition of the highly educated Negro is restricted to becoming principals of the high schools. The neglected state school has not developed sufficiently to become attractive. The warring area, then, is in the cities. In one of them, where several Negroes own considerable wealth which, if pooled and properly used, would produce all but wonderful results, the petty strife has been most disastrous. Little thought is given to social uplift, and economic effort is crushed by factional wrangling. Before the author had been in one of the towns an hour a stalwart of one faction sounded him on becoming a candidate for the position held by the principal of the high school. A few minutes thereafter another approached him for advice as to how "to get him out."

The high cost of this childishness to the community can be estimated only by taking into consideration the fact that this strife is all but endless. If it were a matter that developed now and then only to be forgotten by people directing their attention thereafter to more important things, it would not do much harm; but this confusion continues for years. Sometimes it grips a community for a whole generation, vitiating the entire life of the people.

In spite of the meager rewards, however, the idea of leadership looms high in the Negro mind. It always develops thus among oppressed people. The oppressor must have some dealing with the despised group, and rather than have contact with individuals he approaches the masses through his own spokesman. The term itself connotes a backward condition. In its

strides upward a race shuffles off its leaders because they origi-
nate outside of the group. They constitute a load that sinks the
oppressed in the mire of trials and tribulations.

Leadership is usually superimposed for the purpose of "directing the course of the ostracized group along sane lines."
This was accomplished during the days of slavery by restricting the assembly of Negroes to certain times and places and
compelling them to meet in the presence of a stipulated number of the "wisest and discreetest men of the community."
These supervisors of the conduct of Negroes would prevent
them from learning the truth which might make them "un-
ruly" or ambitious to become free.

After the Negroes became free the same end was reached by
employing a Negro or some white man to spy upon and report
behind closed doors on a plan to enslave the Negroes' minds.
In case that actual employment as a spy seemed too bold, the
person to be used as such an instrument took up some sort of
enterprise which the oppressors of the race warmly supported
to give him the desired influence in the community. This "racial racketeer" might be a politician, minister, teacher, director of a community center, or head of a "social uplift agency."
As long as he did certain things and expressed the popular
opinion on questions he lacked nothing, and those who followed him found their way apparently better paid as the years
went by. His leadership, then, was recognized and the ultimate
undoing of the Negroes in the community was assured.

Such leadership, too, has continued into our day and it goes
from bad to worse. The very service which this racial toady
renders hardens him to the extent that he loses his soul. He becomes equal to any task the oppressor may impose upon him,
and at the same time he becomes artful enough to press his
case convincingly before the thoughtless multitude. What is
right is sacrificed because everything that is right is not expedient; and what is expedient soon becomes unnecessary.

Recently a citizen, observing how we have been thus be-
trayed, suggested that there be called a national meeting to
take steps for a program of development of the race from
within under "a new leadership." Such a movement can be

made to mean something, and then it can degenerate into an assembly of abuse and vituperation followed by the usual whereas-therefore-be-it-resolved effort which has never meant anything in the awakening and the development of an oppressed people.

The Negroes, however, will not advance far if they continue to waste their energy abusing those who misdirect and exploit them. The exploiters of the race are not so much at fault as the race itself. If Negroes persist in permitting themselves to be handled in this fashion they will always find some one at hand to impose upon them. The matter is one which rests largely with the Negroes themselves. The race will free itself from exploiters just as soon as it decides to do so. No one else can accomplish this task for the race. It must plan and do for itself.

Checking up on what they do, Negroes often find themselves giving money and moral support to various persons and institutions which influence the course of the race in the wrong way. They do not often ask themselves whether the support thus given will redound in the long run to the good of the people with whom they are identified. They do not inquire whether the assistance thus given offers temporary relief but eventually results in irreparable loss. So many Negroes often do themselves harm when they actually believe that they are doing good. Under their present teachers they cannot easily learn to do any better, for such training as we undergo does not open our eyes sufficiently for us to see far ahead of us.

If the Negro could abandon the idea of leadership and instead stimulate a larger number of the race to take up definite tasks and sacrifice their time and energy in doing these things efficiently the race might accomplish something. The race needs workers, not leaders. Such workers will solve the problems which race leaders talk about and raise money to enable them to talk more and more about. When you hear a man talking, then, always inquire as to what he is doing or what he has done for humanity. Oratory and resolutions do not avail much. If they did, the Negro race would be in a paradise on earth. It may be well to repeat here the saying that old men talk of what they have done, young men of what they are doing, and fools of what they expect to do. The Negro race has a rather large share of the last mentioned class.

If we can finally succeed in translating the idea of leadership into that of service, we may soon find it possible to lift the Negro to a higher level. Under leadership we have come into the ghetto; by service within the ranks we may work our way out of it. Under leadership we have been constrained to do the biddings of others; by service we may work out a program in the light of our own circumstances. Under leadership we have become poverty-stricken; by service we may teach the masses how to earn a living honestly. Under leadership we have been made to despise our own possibilities and to develop into parasites; by service we may prove sufficient unto the task of self-development and contribute our part to modern culture.

CHAPTER XII

HIRELINGS IN THE PLACES OF PUBLIC SERVANTS

If the highly educated Negroes have not learned better the simple lessons of life one cannot expect the laboring classes to conduct themselves differently. In the large number of cases the employers of Negroes in common labor, in which most of them are now engaged, assert that there is no hope for advancement of Negroes in their employ because Negroes will not work under foremen of their own color. In other words, the average Negro has not yet developed to the point that one is willing to take orders from another of his own race.

While it is true that such an answer is often given as a mere excuse for not placing Negroes in responsible positions when it can be done without any particular trouble, the investigation among Negroes themselves reveals numerous facts to prove that there is more truth than falsehood in this statement. Hundreds of employees of African blood frankly say that they will not work under a Negro. One is afraid that the other may prosper more than he does and be recognized accordingly.

Some of these instances are interesting. A head of one of the Government departments, in which Negro women are employed to do unskilled labor, reports that he placed in charge of the group of these workers an intelligent colored woman who seemed to have all of the necessary qualifications which he had found in other women thus employed. Those working under her, however, refused to obey instructions, kept the place in turmoil and soon destroyed the morale of the whole force. As soon as he placed a white woman in charge, however, order was reestablished on the premises, and everything moved along smoothly.

Another employer conducting a wholesale business placed a Negro foreman in charge of others of his race to function as one of the important departments of the establishment. The Negroes working under him, who had formerly taken orders without question from the white foreman, soon undertook to take liberties with the promoted Negro and to ignore his orders. Knowing that the Negro foreman was well qualified, however, and being personally interested in him, the employer instead of doing what so many others under such circumstances had done, dismissed those who refused to cooperate and supplied the vacancies with others until an efficient working force could thus be obtained. Only a few employers, however, have had such patience and have manifested such interest in the advancement of the Negro. As a rule they merely dispose of Negro foremen with the excuse that one Negro will not take orders from another.

This refusal of Negroes to take orders from one another is due largely to the fact that slaveholders taught their bondmen that they were as good as or better than any others and, therefore, should not be subjected to any member of their race. If they were to be subordinated to some one it should be to the white man of superior culture and social position. This keeps the whole race on a lower level, restricted to the atmosphere of trifles which do not concern their traducers. The greater things of life which can be attained only by wise leadership, then, they have no way to accomplish.

The strong have always used this as a means of dealing with the so-called weaker races of the world. The Caucasian arrays the one against the other so that they may never combine their forces and thus deprive their so-called superiors of control over them, which they could easily do if organized. One white man was thus able to maintain himself on a plantation where there were thirty or forty slaves because the Negroes were mis-educated in such a way as to keep them divided into distinct factions. In petty strife their power would be lost in the process of attrition. Today we find the same thing in Africa where this end is reached by embittering one tribe against another; and it worked the same way in India until recently when it began to break down under the masterful leadership of Mahatma Gandhi.

The Negroes of the United States have followed leadership slavishly but sometimes unfortunately that of those leaders who are selected for them by the traducers of the race. The enemies of the race, for example, will find a Negro willing to do certain things they desire to have accomplished and will finance him and give him sufficient publicity to get before the world, for the few favors which he may dispense among his followers as a result of his influence and economic position will bring to him the adequate number of Negroes for the constituency which he desires.

Negroes, however, sometimes choose their own leaders but unfortunately they are too often of the wrong kind. Negroes do not readily follow persons with constructive programs. Almost any sort of exciting appeal or trivial matter presented to them may receive immediate attention and temporarily at least liberal support. When the bubble collapses, of course, these same followers will begin to decry Negro leadership and call these misrepresentatives of the group rascals and scoundrels. Inasmuch as they have failed to exercise foresight, however, those who have deceived them should not be blamed so much as those who have liberally supported these impostors. Yet the fault here is not inherently in the Negro but in what he has been taught.

The Negroes' point of view, therefore, must be changed before they can construct a program which will bring them out of the wilderness. For example, no good can be expected from one of our teachers who said that she had to give up her class in Sunday school to accept an extra job of waiting on table at that hour because she had bought a twenty-four-hundred-dollar coat and her husband had purchased an expensive car. Such a teacher has no message for the Negro child. Her example would tend to drag the youth downward, and the very thought of having such a person in the schoolroom is most depressing.

We must feel equally discouraged when we see a minister driving up to his church on Sunday morning in a Cadillac. He does not come to feed the multitude spiritually. He comes to fleece the flock. The appeal he makes is usually emotional. While the people are feeling happy the expensive machine is granted, and the prolonged vacation to use it is easily financed. Thus the thoughtless drift backward toward slavery.

When you see a physician drive to one's door in his Pierce Arrow, you cannot get the impression he has come to treat the patient for a complaint. He has come to treat him for a dollar. Such physicians, as a rule, know less and less medicine as the years go by, although they make much money by learning human psychology and using it for personal gain. With leeches of this type feeding upon an all but impoverished people and giving them nothing back there can be no hope for advancement.

No people can go forward when the majority of those who should know better have chosen to go backward, but this is exactly what most of our misleaders do. Not being learned in the history and background of the race, they figure out that there is no hope for the masses; and they decide, then, that the best thing they can do is to exploit these people for all they can and use the accumulations selfishly. Such persons have no vision and therefore perish at their own hands.

It is an injustice to the Negro, however, to mis-educate him and suffer his manners to be corrupted from infancy unto old age and then blame him for making the mistakes which such guidance necessitates. "People who have been restricted and held down naturally condescend to the lower levels of delinquency. When education has been entirely neglected or improperly managed we see the worst passions ruling with uncontrolled and incessant sway. Good sense degenerates into craft, anger wrangles into malignity, restraint which is thought most solitary comes too late, and the most judicial admonitions are urged in vain."

Philosophers have long conceded, however, that every man has two educations: "that which is given to him, and the other that which he gives himself. Of the two kinds the latter is by far the more desirable. Indeed all that is most worthy in man he must work out and conquer for himself. It is that which constitutes our real and best nourishment. What we are merely taught seldom nourishes the mind like that which we teach ourselves."

The same eternal principle applies to a race forced to live apart from others as a separate and distinct group. Inasmuch as the education of the Negro has come from without we can clearly see that he has received only a part of the development which he should have undergone or he has developed negatively. The Negro lacks mental power, which cannot be expected from ill-fed brains.

This naturally brings up a serious question. The people on the outside, who are directing the race from afar, will take this condition of affairs as evidence that the Negro is not prepared for leadership. What they ought to say is that they have not prepared the Negro to assume the responsibility of his own uplift. Instead of doing this, however, they play up this result of their own failure as an argument for imposing upon the Negro race the guidance of others from without.

As to whether or not a white man should be a leader of the Negroes may be dismissed as a silly question. What has the color to do with it? Such a worker may be white, brown, yellow, or red, if he is heart and soul with the people whom he would serve. It just happens, however, that most white men now in control of Negro institutions are not of this required type. Practically all of those with whom I have talked and communicated believe in imposing some sort of disability upon Negroes. Some object to the freedom of intermarriage as a substitute for concubinage, scoff at the idea of the enfranchisement of the Negroes, approve their segregation, and justify the economic exploitation of the race. Now if these are the persons to elevate the Negroes, to what point do they expect to lift them, and what will the Negroes be when they get there?

With this same thought in mind a white director of Negroes recently said to the author:

"I realize that I have no useful function in my present position as a president of a Negro institution. I do not approve of their aspirations to many things. I cannot accept the students in my house as I would white students because it might lead to an interracial romance. Marrying is such a difficult problem at the best that I should not like to see one of my children make a failure in life by marrying a Negro.

"In other words," continued he, "we live in two different worlds. While I am among them I cannot become a part of them. How then can I help them under these circumstances?"

I am acquainted with another white educator at the head of a Negro institution, who will not address a colored girl as Miss, and to avoid the use of a title in speaking to women of the race he addresses them as his kin. One of them was sharp enough to reply to him thus when he accosted her as auntie:

"Oh, I am so glad that I have found my lost relatives at last. My mother often told me that I had some distinguished kin, and just to think that you are my nephew makes me feel glad."

Another such exploiter in charge of a Negro college never wears his hat on the campus. His confidential explanation is that he might have to lift it when he meets a Negro woman. Of course, that would never do. "White supremacy" would be lost in the Negro school.

As we realize more and more that education is not merely imparting information which is expected to produce certain results, we see very clearly the inconsistency of the position of white persons as executives of Negro institutions. These misfits belong to the very group working out the segregation of the Negro, and they come into these institutions mainly to earn a living. They make no particular contribution to the development of education, for they are not scholarly enough to influence educational theory; and they are so far out of sympathy with the Negro that they cannot make any contribution to educational practice. These "foreigners" are not bringing to such institutions large sums of money which the Negroes cannot obtain, for the institutions now directed by Negroes are receiving larger appropriations than those under the management of whites.

Our so-called thinkers, however, seldom see the inevitable results of this unsound policy. Not long ago when the author wrote the textbook entitled *Negro Makers of History* it was adversely criticised by a Negro who said that the book should have had as an illustration the cut of the white man who established a certain Negro college. The author had to explain that the book was to give an account of what the Negro has done, not of what has been done for him.

The school referred to, moreover, was in no sense a Negro school. It had very few Negro teachers and only one Negro trustee. The policy of the school was determined altogether by others without giving the Negro credit for having a thought on education. In other words, it was merely a school which Negroes were permitted to attend. If they picked up here and there something to help them, well and good; if not, may God help them!

It is all right to have a white man as the head of a Negro college or to have a red man at the head of a yellow one, if in each case the incumbent has taken out his naturalization papers and has identified himself as one of the group which he is trying to serve. It seems that the white educators of this day are unwilling to do this, and for that reason they can never contribute to the actual development of the Negro from within. You cannot serve people by giving them orders as to what to do. The real servant of the people must live among them, think with them, feel for them, and die for them.

The white worker in Negro institutions, too, can never be successful without manifesting some faith in the people with whom he has cast his lot. His efforts must not be merely an attempt to stimulate their imitation of things in a foreign sphere. He must study his community sufficiently to discover the things which have a trend in the proper direction that he may stimulate such forces and thus help the community to do better the good things which it may be capable of doing and at the same time may be interested in doing. If these people are to be brought the ideas of "foreigners," and must be miraculously transformed into something else before anything can be made of them, such effort will be a fruitless task like most of the so-called education and uplift of the Negroes in America.

The Negro, in spite of his confinement to the ghetto, has

some opportunities to develop his special capacities if they are properly studied and understood. The real servant of the people, then, will give more attention to those to be served than to the use that somebody may want to make of them. He will be more concerned with what he can do to increase the ease, comfort, and happiness of the Negro than with how the Negro may be used to contribute to the ease, comfort, and happiness of others.

The servant of the people, unlike the leader, is not on a high horse elevated above the people and trying to carry them to some designated point to which he would like to go for his own advantage. The servant of the people is down among them, living as they live, doing what they do and enjoying what they enjoy. He may be a little better informed than some other members of the group; it may be that he has had some experience that they have not had, but in spite of this advantage he should have more humility than those whom he serves, for we are told that "Whosoever is greatest among you, let him be your servant."

CHAPTER XIII

UNDERSTAND THE NEGRO

"We do not offer here any course in Negro history, Negro literature, or race relations," recently said a professor of a Negro college. "We study the Negro along with other people."

"An excellent idea," the interviewer replied. "No one should expect you to do any more than this, but how do you do it when the Negro is not mentioned in your textbooks except to be condemned? Do you, a teacher in a Negro school, also condemn the race in the same fashion as the writers of your textbooks of history and literature?"

"No," said he, "we bring the Negro in here and there."

"How often does 'here and there' connote?"

"Well, you know," said he, "Negroes have not done much; and what they have accomplished may be briefly covered by referring to the achievements of a few men and women.

"Why do you emphasize the special study of the Negro?" said he further. "Why is it necessary to give the race special attention in the press, on the rostrum, or in the schoolroom? This idea of projecting the Negro into the foreground does the race much harm by singing continually of his woes and problems and thus alienating the public which desires to give its attention to other things."

It is true that many Negroes do not desire to hear anything about their race, and few whites of today will listen to the story of woe. With most of them the race question has been settled. The Negro has been assigned to the lowest drudgery as the sphere in which the masses must toil to make a living; and socially and politically the race has been generally proscribed. Inasmuch as the traducers of the race have "settled" the matter in this fashion, they naturally oppose any effort to change this status.

Many Negro professional men who are making a living attending to the affairs of these laborers and servants in their mentally undeveloped state and many teachers who in conservative fashion are instructing their children to maintain the *status quo ante bellum*, also oppose any movement to upset this arrangement. They are getting paid for their efforts. Why should they try innovations? The gods have so decreed it. Human beings cannot change it. Why be foolish?

A Negro with sufficient thought to construct a program of his own is undesirable, and the educational systems of this country generally refuse to work through such Negroes in promoting their cause. The program for the uplift of the Negroes in this country must be handed over to an executive force like orders from the throne, and they must carry it out without question or get out of line and let the procession go on. Although the Negro is being daily forced more and more by segregation into a world peculiarly his own, his unusually perplexing status is given little or no thought, and he is not considered capable of thinking for himself.

The chief difficulty with the education of the Negro is that it has been largely imitation resulting in the enslavement of his mind. Somebody outside of the race has desired to try out on Negroes some experiment which interested him and his co-workers; and Negroes, being objects of charity, have received them cordially and have done what they required. In fact, the keynote in the education of the Negro has been to do what he is told to do. Any Negro who has learned to do this is well prepared to function in the American social order as others would have him.

Looking over the courses of study of the public schools, one finds little to show that the Negro figures in these curricula. In supplementary matter a good deed of some Negro is occasionally referred to, but oftener the race is mentioned only to be held up to ridicule. With the exception of a few places like Atlantic City, Atlanta, Tulsa, St. Louis, Birmingham, Knoxville, and the states of Louisiana and North Carolina no effort is made to study the Negro in the public schools as they do the Latin, the Teuton, or the Mongolian. Several mis-educated Negroes themselves contend that the study of the Negro by children would bring before them the race problem prematurely and, therefore, urge that the study of the race be deferred until they reach advanced work in the college or university. These misguided teachers ignore the fact that the race question is being brought before black and white children daily in their homes, in the streets, through the press and on the rostrum. How, then, can the school ignore the duty of teaching the truth while these other agencies are playing up falsehood?

The experience of college instructors shows that racial attitudes of the youth are not easily changed after they reach adolescence. Although students of this advanced stage are shown the fallacy of race superiority and the folly of social distinctions, they nevertheless continue to do the illogical thing of still looking upon these depised groups as less worthy than themselves and persist in treating them accordingly. Teachers of elementary and secondary schools giving attention to this interracial problem have succeeded in softening and changing the attitude of children whose judgment has not been so hopelessly warped by the general attitude of the communities in which they have been brought up.

In approaching this problem in this fashion to counteract the one-sided education of youth the thinking people of this country have no desire to upset the curricula of the schools or to force the Negro as such into public discussion; but, if the Negro is to be elevated he must be educated in the sense of being developed from what he is, and the public must be so enlightened as to think of the Negro as a man. Furthermore, no one can be thoroughly educated until he learns as much about the Negro as he knows about other people.

Upon examining the recent catalogues of the leading Negro colleges, one finds that invariably they give courses in ancient, medieval, and modern Europe, but they do not give such courses in ancient, mediæval, and modern Africa. Yet Africa, according to recent discoveries, has contributed about as much

to the progress of mankind as Europe has, and the early civilization of the Mediterranean world was decidedly influenced
by Africa.

Negro colleges offer courses bearing on the European colonists prior to their coming to America, their settlement on
these shores, and their development here toward independence. Why are they not equally generous with the Negroes in
treating their status in Africa prior to enslavement, their first
transplantation to the West Indies, the Latinization of certain
Negroes in contradistinction to the development of others
under the influence of the Teuton, and the effort of the race toward self-expression?

A further examination of their curricula shows, too, that invariably these Negro colleges offer courses in Greek philosophy and in that of modern European thought, but they direct
no attention to the philosophy of the African. Negroes of Africa have and always have had their own ideas about the nature of the universe, time, and space, about appearance and
reality, and about freedom and necessity. The effort of the
Negro to interpret man's relation to the universe shows just as
much intelligence as we find in the philosophy of the Greeks.
There were many Africans who were just as wise as Socrates.

Again, one observes in some of these catalogues numerous
courses in art but no well defined course in Negro or African
art which early influenced that of the Greeks. Thinkers are
now saying that the early culture of the Mediterranean was
chiefly African. Most of these colleges do not even direct special attention to Negro music in which the Negro has made his
outstanding contribution in America. The unreasonable attitude is that because the whites do not have these things in
their schools the Negroes must not have them in theirs. The
Catholics and Jews, therefore, are wrong in establishing special schools to teach their principles of religion, and the Germans in America are unwise in having their children taught
their mother tongue.

Such has been the education of Negroes. They have been
taught facts of history, but have never learned to think. Their
conception is that you go to school to find out what other

people have done, and then you go out in life to imitate them. What they have done can be done by others, they contend; and they are right. They are wrong, however, in failing to realize that what others have done, we may not need to do. If we are to do identically the same thing from generation to generation, we would not make any progress. If we are to duplicate from century to century the same feats, the world will grow tired of such a monotonous performance.

In this particular respect "Negro education" is a failure, and disastrously so, because in its present predicament the race is especially in need of vision and invention to give humanity something new. The world does not want and will never have the heroes and heroines of the past. What this age needs is an enlightened youth not to undertake the tasks like theirs but to imbibe the spirit of these great men and answer the present call of duty with equal nobleness of soul.

Not only do the needs of generations vary, but the individuals themselves are not duplicates the one of the other; and being different in this respect, their only hope to function efficiently in society is to know themselves and the generation which they are to serve. The chief value in studying the records of others is to become better acquainted with oneself and with one's possibilities to live and to do in the present age. As long as Negroes continue to restrict themselves to doing what was necessary a hundred or a thousand years ago, they must naturally expect to be left out of the great scheme of things as they concern men of today.

The most inviting field for discovery and invention, then, is the Negro himself, but he does not realize it. Fredrika Bremer,[1] when reflecting upon her visit to America about 1850, gave this country a new thought in saying to Americans, "The romance of your history is the fate of the Negro." In this very thought lies unusual possibilities for the historian, the economist, the artist, and the philosopher. Why should the Negro writer seek a theme abroad when he has the greatest of all at home?

The bondage of the Negro brought captive from Africa is one of the greatest dramas in history, and the writer who merely sees in that ordeal something to approve or condemn fails to understand the evolution of the human race. Negroes now studying dramatics go into our schools to reproduce Shakespeare, but mentally developed members of this race would see the possibilities of a greater drama in the tragedy of the man of color. Negroes graduating from conservatories of music dislike the singing of our folk songs. For some reason such misguided persons think that they can improve on the productions of the foreign drama or render the music of other people better than they can themselves.

A knowledge of real history would lead one to think that slavery was one of the significant developments which, although evil in themselves, may redound sometimes to the advantage of the oppressed rather than to that of the oppressor. Some one has said that the music of Poland was inspired by incidents of a struggle against the despots invading and partitioning their prostrate land. The Greeks never had an art until the country was overrun by hostile Orientals. Some one then began to immortalize in song the sons who went forth to fight for the native land. Another carved in marble the thought evoked by the example of the Greek youth who blocked the mountain pass with his body or who bared his breast to the javelin to defend the liberty of his country. These things we call art.

In our own country the other elements of the population, being secure in their position, have never faced such a crisis; and the Europeans, after whose pattern American life is fashioned, have not recently had such experience. White Americans, then, have produced no art at all, and that of Europe has reached the point of stagnation. Negroes who are imitating whites, then, are engaged in a most unprofitable performance. Why not interpret themselves anew to the world?

If we had a few thinkers we could expect great achievements on tomorrow. Some Negro with unusual insight would write an epic of bondage and freedom which would take its place with those of Homer and Virgil. Some Negro with esthetic appreciation would construct from collected fragments of Negro music a grand opera that would move humanity to repentance.

Some Negro of philosophic penetration would find a solace for the modern world in the soul of the Negro, and then men would be men because they are men.

The Negro in his present plight, however, does not see possibilities until it is too late. He exercises much "hindsight," and for that reason he loses ground in the hotly contested battles of life. The Negro as a rule waits until a thing happens before he tries to avert it. He is too much like a man whom the author once saw knocked down in a physical combat. Instead of dodging the blow when it was being dealt he arose from his prostration dodging it.

For example, the author has just received a letter from a lady in Pittsburgh complaining that the librarian in one of its schools insists upon reading to the children "a great deal of literature containing such words as 'nigger,' 'Blackie,' 'Little Black Sambo,' etc." This lady, therefore, would like to place in that school some books by Negro authors. This is a commendable effort, but it comes a little late; we hope not too late.

For centuries such literature has been circulated among the children of the modern world; and they have, therefore, come to regard the Negro as inferior. Now that some of our similarly mis-educated Negroes are seeing how they have been deceived they are awakening to address themselves to a long neglected work. They should have been thinking about this generations ago, for they have a tremendous task before them today in dispelling this error and counteracting the results of such bias in our literature.

There has just come, too, from a friend of humanity in Edinburgh, Scotland, a direful account of the increase in race prejudice in those parts. Sailors who had frequented the stronghold of race prejudice in South Africa undertook recently to prevent Negro men from socializing with Scotch women at a dance; and certain professors of the University of Edinburgh with the same attitude show so much of it in their teaching that this friend entreats us to send them informing books on the Negro. We are doing it.

Here again, however, the effort to uproot error and popularize the truth comes rather late. The Negro since freedom has gone along grinning, whooping, and "cutting capers" while the white man has applied himself to the task of defining the status of the Negro and compelling him to accept it as thus settled forever. While the Negro has been idle, propaganda has gone far ahead of history. Unfortunately, too, Negro "scholars" have assisted in the production of literature which gives this point of view.

CHAPTER XIV

THE NEW PROGRAM

It seems only a reasonable proposition, then, that, if under the present system which produced our leadership in religion, politics, and business we have gone backward toward serfdom or have at least been kept from advancing to real freedom, it is high time to develop another sort of leadership with a different educational system. In the first place, we must bear in mind that the Negro has never been educated. He has merely been informed about other things which he has not been permitted to do. The Negroes have been shoved out of the regular schools through the rear door into the obscurity of the backyard and told to imitate others whom they see from afar, or they have been permitted in some places to come into the public schools to see how others educate themselves. The program for the uplift of the Negro in this country must be based upon a scientific study of the Negro from within to develop in him the power to do for himself what his oppressors will never do to elevate him to the level of others.

Being without actual education, we have very few persons prepared to help the Negroes whom they have set out to lead. These persons are not all dishonest men and women. Many of them are sincere, and believe that they are doing the race some great good in thus holding it backward. They must be awakened and shown the error of their ways.

We have very few teachers because most of those with whom we are afflicted know nothing about the children whom they teach or about their parents who influence the pupils more than the teachers themselves. When a boy comes to school without knowing his lesson he should be studied instead of being punished. The boy who does well in the beginning of the year and lags behind near the end of the term should not always be censured or ridiculed. As a rule, such children are not responsible for their failures. Their parents and their social status account mainly for these shortcomings. The Negro teacher, then, must treat the disease rather than its symptoms.

But can you expect teachers to revolutionize the social order for the good of the community? Indeed we must expect this very thing. The educational system of a country is worthless unless it accomplishes this task. Men of scholarship and consequently of prophetic insight must show us the right way and lead us into the light which shines brighter and brighter.

In the church where we have much freedom and independence we must get rid of preachers who are not prepared to help the people whom they exploit. The public must refuse to support men of this type. Ministers who are the creations of the old educational system must be awakened, and if this is impossible they must be dethroned. Those who keep the people in ignorance and play upon their emotions must be exiled. The people have never been taught what religion is, for most of the preachers find it easier to stimulate the superstition which develops in the unenlightened mind. Religion in such hands, then, becomes something with which you take advantage of weak people. Why try to enlighten the people in such matters when superstition serves just as well for exploitation?

The ministers with the confidence of the people must above all things understand the people themselves. They must find out the past of their parishioners, whether they were brought up in Georgia, Alabama or Texas, whether they are housed under desirable circumstances, what they do to make a living, what they do with their earnings, how they react to the world about them, how they spend their leisure, or how they function along with other elements of the social order.

In our schools, and especially in schools of religion, attention should be given to the study of the Negro as he developed during the antebellum period by showing to what extent that remote culture was determined by ideas which the Negro brought with him from Africa. To take it for granted that the antebellum Negro was an ignoramus or that the native brought from Africa had not a valuable culture merely because some prejudiced writers have said so does not show the attitude of scholarship, and Negro students who direct their courses accordingly will never be able to grapple with the social problems presented today by the Negro church.

The preachers of today must learn to do as well as those of old. Richard Allen so interpreted Christianity anew to his master that he was converted, and so did Henry Evans and George Bentley for other whites in North Carolina and Tennessee.[1] Instead of accepting and trying to carry out the theories which the exploiters of humanity have brought them for a religious program the Negroes should forget their differences and in the strength of a united church bring out a new interpretation of Christ to this unwilling world. Following the religious teachings of their traducers, the Negroes do not show any more common sense than a people would in permitting criminals to enact the laws and establish the procedure of the courts by which they are to be tried.

Negro preachers, too, must be educated to their people rather than away from them. This, of course, requires a new type of religious school. To provide for such training the Negro church must get rid of its burdensome supervisory force. If the number of bishops of the various Negro Methodist churches were reduced to about twelve or fifteen, as they should be, the amount of a hundred thousand dollars or more now being paid to support the unnecessary number could be used to maintain properly at least one accredited college; and what is now being raised here and there to support various struggling but starving institutions kept alive by ambitious bishops and preachers could be saved to the people. With this money diverted to a more practical use the race would be able to establish some other things which would serve as assets rather than as liabilities.

We say liabilities, for practically all of our denominational schools which are bleeding the people for the inadequate support which they receive are still unable to do accredited work. There are so many of them that the one impoverishes the other.

Outstanding men of the church, therefore, have to acquire their advanced education by attending other schools in the beginning or by taking additional training elsewhere after learning all our denominational schools can offer. This is a loss of ground which should be regained if the church is to go forward.

By proper unification and organization the Negro churches might support one or two much needed universities of their own. With the present arrangement of two or three in the same area and sometimes as many in one city there is no chance for emerging from the trying poverty-stricken state. And even if these institutions could do well what they undertake they do not supply all educational needs. To qualify for certification in the professions Negroes must go to other schools, where, although they acquire the fundamentals, they learn much about their "inferiority" to discourage them in their struggle upward.

We should not close any accredited Negro colleges or universities, but we should reconstruct the whole system. We should not eliminate many of the courses now being offered, but we should secure men of vision to give them from the point of view of the people to be served. We should not spend less money for the higher education of the Negro, but should redefine higher education as preparation to think and work out a program to serve the lowly rather than to live as an aristocrat.

Such subjects of certitude as mathematics, of course, would continue and so would most of the work in practical languages and science. In theology, literature, social science, and education, however, radical reconstruction is necessary. The old worn-out theories as to man's relation to God and his fellow man, the system of thought which has permitted one man to exploit, oppress, and exterminate another and still be regarded as righteous must be discarded for the new thought of men as brethren and the idea of God as the lover of all mankind.

After Negro students have mastered the fundamentals of English, the principles of composition, and the leading facts in the development of its literature, they should not spend all of their time in advanced work on Shakespeare, Chaucer and Anglo-Saxon. They should direct their attention also to the folklore of the African, to the philosophy in his proverbs, to the development of the Negro in the use of modern language, and to the works of Negro writers.

The leading facts of the history of the world should be studied by all, but of what advantage is it to the Negro student of history to devote all of his time to courses bearing on such despots as Alexander the Great, Caesar, and Napoleon, or to the record of those nations whose outstanding achievement has been rapine, plunder, and murder for world power? Why not study the African background from the point of view of anthropology and history, and then take up sociology as it concerns the Negro peasant or proletarian who is suffering from sufficient ills to supply laboratory work for the most advanced students of the social order? Why not take up economics as reflected by the Negroes of today and work out some remedy for their lack of capital, the absence of cooperative enterprise, and the short life of their establishments. Institutions like Harvard, Yale and Columbia are not going to do these things, and educators influenced by them to the extent that they become blind to the Negro will never serve the race efficiently.

To educate the Negro we must find out exactly what his background is, what he is today, what his possibilities are, how to begin with him as he is and make him a better individual of the kind that he is. Instead of cramming the Negro's mind with what others have shown that they can do, we should develop his latent powers that he may perform in society a part of which others are not capable.

During his life the author has seen striking examples of how people should and should not be taught. Some of these are worth relating. Probably the most interesting was that of missionary work in China. In 1903 the author crossed the Pacific Ocean with twenty-six missionaries who were going to take the Orient by storm. One Todd, from North Carolina, was orating and preaching almost every day to stimulate his coworkers to go boldly to the task before them. Dr. De Forest, long a missionary to Japan, informed them that the work required more than enthusiasm; that they could not rush into the homes of the natives saying, "Peace be to this house," for it might turn out the other way and give somebody the opportunity to say, "Peace be to his ashes."

Dr. De Forest explained to them how he chose a decidedly different course, preferring first to study the history, the language, the manners and the customs of the people to approach them intelligently; and not until he had been in the country four years did he undertake to exhort, but after that time he had had great success and had been invited to preach before the Mikado himself. Now Todd did not take this advice, and he had not been in China five months before he and his wife had been poisoned by their native cook who had become incensed at the way they interfered with the institutions of his people.

Another striking illustration was the education of the Filipinos. Not long after the close of the Spanish-American War the United States Government started out to educate the Filipinos over night. Numbers of "highly trained" Americans were carried there to do the work. They entered upon their task by teaching the Filipinos just as they had taught American children who were otherwise circumstanced. The result was failure. Men trained at institutions like Harvard, Yale, Columbia, and Chicago could not reach these people and had to be dismissed from the service. Some of these "scholarly" Americans had to be maintained by the subscription of friends until they could be returned to this country on Government transportation.

In the meantime, however, there came along an insurance man, who went to the Philippines to engage in business. He had never taught at all, and he had never studied authorities like Bagley, Judd, and Thorndike;[2] but he understood people. Seeing that others had failed, he went into the work himself. He filled the schoolroom with thousands of objects from the pupil's environment. In the beginning he did not use books very much, because those supplied were not adapted to the needs of the children. He talked about the objects around them. Everything was presented objectively. When he took up the habits of the snake he brought the reptile to the school for demonstration. When he taught the crocodile he had one there. In teaching the Filipinos music he did not sing "Come shake the Apple-Tree." They had never seen such an object. He taught them to sing "Come shake the Lomboy Tree," something which they had actually done. In reading he did not concentrate on the story of how George Washington always told the truth. They had never heard of him and could not have appreciated that myth if some one had told them about it. This real educator taught them about their own hero, José Rizal,[3] who gave his life as a martyr for the freedom of his country. By and by they got rid of most books based on the life of American people and worked out an entirely new series dealing with the life of Filipinos. The result, then, was that this man and others who saw the situation as he did succeeded, and the work of the public schools in the Philippines is today the outstanding achievement of the Americans in that country.

We do not mean to suggest here, however, that any people should ignore the record of the progress of other races. We would not advocate any such unwise course. We say, hold on to the real facts of history as they are, but complete such knowledge by studying also the history of races and nations which have been purposely ignored. We should not underrate the achievements of Mesopotamia, Greece, and Rome; but we should give equally as much attention to the internal African kingdoms, the Songhay empire, and Ethiopia, which through Egypt decidedly influenced the civilization of the Mediterranean world. We would not ignore the rise of Christianity and the development of the Church; but we would at the same time give honorable mention to the persons of African blood who figured in these achievements, and who today are endeavoring to carry out the principles of Jesus long since repudiated by most so-called Christians. We would not underestimate the achievements of the captains of industry who in the commercial expansion of the modern world have produced the wealth necessary to ease and comfort; but we would give credit to the Negro who so largely supplied the demand for labor by which these things have been accomplished.

In our own particular history we would not dim one bit the lustre of any star in our firmament. We would not learn less of

George Washington, "First in War, First in Peace and First in the Hearts of his Countrymen"; but we would learn something also of the three thousand Negro soldiers of the American Revolution who helped to make this "Father of our Country" possible. We would not neglect to appreciate the unusual contribution of Thomas Jefferson to freedom and democracy; but we would invite attention also to two of his outstanding contemporaries, Phillis Wheatley, the writer of interesting verse, and Benjamin Banneker, the mathematician, astronomer, and advocate of a world peace plan set forth in 1793 with the vital principles of Woodrow Wilson's League of Nations. We would in no way detract from the fame of Perry on Lake Erie or Jackson at New Orleans in the second struggle with England; but we would remember the gallant black men who assisted in winning these memorable victories on land and sea. We would not cease to pay tribute to Abraham Lincoln as the "Savior of the Country"; but we would ascribe praise also to the one hundred and seventy-eight thousand Negroes who had to be mustered into the service of the Union before it could be preserved, and who by their heroism demonstrated that they were entitled to freedom and citizenship.

CHAPTER XV

VOCATIONAL GUIDANCE

But how can the Negro in this new system learn to make a living, the most important task to which all people must give attention? In view of the Negro's economic plight most of the schools are now worked up over what is called "vocational guidance" in an effort to answer this very question. To what, however, are they to guide their Negro students? Most Negroes now employed are going down blind alleys, and unfortunately some schools seem to do no more than to stimulate their going in that direction.

This may seem to be a rash statement, but a study of our educational system shows that our schools are daily teaching Negroes what they can never apply in life or what is no longer profitable because of the revolution of industry by the multiplication of mechanical appliances. For example, some of our schools are still teaching individual garment making which offers no future today except in catering to the privileged and rich classes. Some of these institutions still offer instruction in shoemaking when the technique developed under their handicaps makes impossible competition with that of the modern factory based upon the invention of a Negro, Jan Matzeliger.[1]

These facts have been known for generations, but some of these institutions apparently change not. Education, like religion, is conservative. It makes haste slowly only, and sometimes not at all. Do not change the present order of thinking and doing, many say, for you disturb too many things long since regarded as ideal. The dead past, according to this view, must be the main factor in determining the future. We should learn from the living past, but let the dead past remain dead.

A survey of employment of the Negroes in this country shows a most undesirable situation. The education of the masses has not enabled them to advance very far in making a living and has not developed in the Negro the power to change this condition. It is revealed that in many establishments the Negro when a young man starts as a janitor or porter and dies in old age in the same position. Tradition fixes his status as such, and both races feel satisfied.

When this janitor or porter dies the dailies headline the passing of this Negro who knew his place and rendered satisfactory service in it. "Distinguished" white men, for whom he ran errands and cleaned cuspidors, volunteer as honorary pall-bearers and follow his remains to the final resting place. Thoughtless Negro editors, instead of expressing their regret that such a life of usefulness was not rewarded by promotion, take up the refrain as some great honor bestowed upon the race.

Among people thus satisfied in the lower pursuits of life and sending their children to school to memorize theories which they never see applied, there can be no such thing as vocational guidance. Such an effort implies an objective; and in the present plight of economic dependence there is no occupation for which the Negro may prepare himself with the assurance that he will find employment. Opportunities which he has today may be taken from him tomorrow; and schools changing their curricula in hit-and-miss fashion may soon find themselves on the wrong track just as they have been for generations.

Negroes do not need some one to guide them to what persons of another race have developed. They must be taught to think and develop something for themselves. It is most pathetic to see Negroes begging others for a chance as we have been doing recently. "Do not force us into starvation," we said. "Let us come into your stores and factories and do a part of what you are doing to profit by our trade." The Negro as a slave developed this fatal sort of dependency; and, restricted mainly to menial service and drudgery during nominal freedom, he has not grown out of it. Now the Negro is facing the ordeal of either learning to do for himself or to die out gradually in the bread line in the ghetto.

If the schools really mean to take a part in necessary uplift they must first supply themselves with teachers. Unfortunately we have very few such workers. The large majority of persons supposedly teaching Negroes never carry to the schoolroom any thought as to improving their condition. From the point of view of these so-called teachers they have done their duty when in automaton fashion they impart in the schoolroom the particular facts which they wrote out in the examination when they "qualified" for their respective positions. Most of them are satisfied with receiving their pay and spending it for the toys and gewgaws of life.

For example, the author is well acquainted with a Negro of this type, who is now serving as the head of one of the largest schools in the United States. From the point of view of our present system he is well educated. He holds advanced degrees from one of the leading institutions of the world; and he is known to be well informed on all the educational theories developed from the time of Socrates down to the day of Dewey. Yet this "educator" says repeatedly that in his daily operations he never has anything to do with Negroes because they are impossible. He says that he never buys anything from a Negro store, and he would not dare to put a penny in a Negro bank.

From such teachers large numbers of Negroes learn this fateful lesson. For example, not long ago a committee of Negroes in a large city went to the owner of a chain store in their neighborhood and requested that he put a Negro manager in charge. This man replied that he doubted that the Negroes themselves wanted such a thing. The Negroes urging him to make the change assured him that they were unanimously in favor of it. The manager, however, asked them to be fair enough with his firm and themselves to investigate before pressing the matter any further. They did so and discovered that one hundred thirty-seven Negro families in that neighborhood seriously objected to buying from Negroes and using articles handled by them. These Negroes, then, had to do the groundwork of uprooting the inferiority idea which had resulted from their mis-education.

To what, then, can a Negro while despising the enterprise of

his fellows guide the youth of his race; and where do you figure out that the youth thus guided will be by 1950? The whites
are daily informing Negroes that they need not come to them
for opportunities. Can the Negro youth, mis-educated by persons who depreciate their efforts, learn to make opportunities
for themselves? This is the real problem which the Negroes
must solve; and he who is not interested in it and makes no effort to solve it is worthless in the present struggle.

Our advanced teachers, like "most highly educated" Negroes, pay little attention to the things about them except
when the shoe begins to pinch on one or the other side. Unless
they happen to become naked they never think of the production of cotton or wool; unless they get hungry they never give
any thought to the output of wheat or corn; unless their friends
lose their jobs they never inquire about the outlook for coal or
steel, or how these things affect the children whom they are
trying to teach. In other words, they live in a world, but they
are not of it. How can such persons guide the youth without
knowing how these things affect the Negro community?

The Negro community, in a sense, is composed of those
around you, but it functions in a different way. You cannot see
it by merely looking out of the windows of the schoolroom.
This community requires scientific investigation. While persons of African blood are compelled to sustain closer relation
to their own people than to other elements in society, they are
otherwise influenced socially and economically. The Negro
community suffers for lack of delimitation because of the various ramifications of life in the United States. For example,
there may be a Negro grocer in the neighborhood, but the
Negro chauffeur for a rich man down town and the washerwoman for an aristocratic family in "quality row" will be more
than apt to buy their food and clothing at the larger establishment with which their employers have connections, although
they may be insulted there. Negroes of the District of Columbia have millions of dollars deposited in banks down town,
where Negro women are not allowed in the ladies' rest rooms.

Right in the heart of the highly educated Negro section of
Washington, too, is a restaurant catering through the front

door exclusively to the white business men, who must live in the Negroes' section to supply them with the necessities of life, and catering at the same time through the back door to numbers of Negroes who pile into that dingy room to purchase whatever may be thrown at them. Yet less than two blocks away are several Negroes running cafés where they can be served for the same amount and under desirable circumstances. Negroes who do this, we say, do not have the proper attitude toward life and its problems, and for that reason we do not take up time with them. They do not belong to our community. The traducers of the race, however, are guiding these people the wrong way. Why do not the "educated" Negroes change their course by identifying themselves with the masses?

For similar reasons the Negro professional man may not always have a beautiful home and a fine car. His plight to the contrary may result from action like that of a poor man who recently knocked on the author's door about midnight to use his telephone to call the ambulance of the Casualty Hospital to take immediate charge of his sick wife. Although living nearer to the Freedmen's Hospital, where more sympathetic consideration would have been given this patient, he preferred to take her to the other hospital where she would have to be carried through the backyard and placed in a room over a stable. He worked there, however; and because of long association with his traducers and the sort of treatment that they have meted out to him he was willing to entrust to their hands the very delicate matter of the health of his wife. This was a part of his community.

Large numbers of Negroes live in such a community. You say that such an atmosphere is not congenial and you will not lose time with these people who are thus satisfied, but the exploiting preacher, the unprincipled politician, the notorious gambler, and the agent of vice are all there purposely misleading these people who have not as yet shaken from their minds the shackles of slavery. What is going to become of them? What is going to become of you?

We avoid them because we find enjoyment among others; but they are developing their own community. Their teacher lives in another community which may or may not be growing. Will his community so expand as to include theirs? If not, their community may encroach upon his. It is a sort of social dualism. What will the end be? The teacher will help to answer this question.

Such guidance, however, must not be restricted to the so-called common people. So many Negroes now engaged in business have no knowledge of its possibilities and limitations. Most of them are as unwise as a Negro business man who came to Washington recently in a ten-thousand-dollar car representing a firm with only one hundred thousand dollars invested. It is only a matter of time before his firm will be no more. He started out destroying his business at the very source. While Negroes are thus spending their means and themselves in riotous living the foreigners come to dwell among them in modest circumstances long enough to get rich and to join those who close in on these unfortunates economically until all the hopes for their redemption are lost.

If the Negroes of this country are to escape starvation and rise out of poverty unto comfort and ease, they must change their way of thinking and living. Never did the author see a more striking demonstration of such a necessity than recently when a young man came to him looking for a job. He was well bedecked with jewelry and fine clothes, and while he was in the office he smoked almost enough cigars to pay one's board for that day. A man of this type in a poverty-stricken group must suffer and die.

A young woman recently displaced in a position from which she received considerable income for a number of years approached the author not long ago to help her solve the problem of making a living. He could not feel very sympathetic toward her, however, for she had on a coat which cost enough to maintain one comfortably for at least two years. While talking with him, moreover, she was so busy telling him about what she wanted that she had little time to inform him as to what she can do to supply her needs.

A man whom the author knows is decidedly handicapped by having lost a lucrative position. He must now work for a little more than half of what he has been accustomed to earn. With

Items Out Receipt

Harold Washington Library Center
Wednesday, December 27, 2023
4:33:35 PM

Item:R0466300810
Title:The mis-education of the Negro
Material:Trade Paperback
Due:1/17/2024 11:59:59 PM
Renewals left:15

Total items:1

Thank you.

his former stipend he was able to maintain two or three girls in addition to his wife, and he drank the best of bootleg stuff available. In now trying to do all of these things on a small wage he finds himself following a most tortuous course to make his ends meet, and he suffers within as well as without.

This undesirable attitude toward life results from the fact that the Negro has learned from others how to spend money much more rapidly than he has learned how to earn it. During these days, therefore, it will be very wise for Negroes to concentrate on the wise use of money and the evil results from the misuse of it. In large cities like Washington, Baltimore, Philadelphia, New York, and Chicago they earn millions and millions every year and throw these vast sums immediately away for trifles which undermine their health, vitiate their morals, and contribute to the undoing of generations of Negroes unborn.

This enlightenment as to economic possibilities in the Negro community must not only include instruction as to how enterprises can be made possible but how they should be apportioned among the various parts of the Negro community. Such knowledge is especially necessary in the case of Negroes because of the fatal tendency toward imitation not only of the white man but the imitation of others in his own group. For example, a Negro starts a restaurant on a corner and does well. Another Negro, observing this prosperity, thinks that he can do just as well by opening a similar establishment next door. The inevitable result is that by dividing the trade between himself and his forerunner he makes it impossible for either one to secure sufficient patronage to continue in business.

In undertakings of great importance this same undesirable tendency toward duplication of effort is also apparent. It has been a common thing to find two or three banks in a Negro community, each one struggling for an existence in competing for the patronage of the small group of people, all of whom would hardly be able to support one such financial institution. These banks continue their unprofitable competition and never think of merging until some crisis forces them to the point that they have to do so or go into bankruptcy. The Negro community, then, never has a strong financial institution with sufficient resources to stimulate the efforts of the business men who otherwise might succeed.

The same shortsightedness has been evident in the case of the insurance companies organized by Negroes. One was established here and then another followed there in imitation of the first. We have been accustomed to boast that the Negroes have about fifty insurance companies in this country, marking the corners of the streets of the cities with large signs displaying what they are doing for the race. Instead of boasting of such unwise expansion we should have received such information with sorrow, for what the race actually needs is to merge all of the insurance companies now supported by Negroes and make one good one. Such a step away from duplication would be a long stride toward our much needed awakening, and it would certainly give us prestige in the business world.

This imitation and duplication are decidedly disastrous to economic enterprise as we can daily observe. A few days ago a young man in the East lamented the fact that after investing his life's earnings in the drug business and making every effort to stimulate the enterprise, he has failed. Some one took occasion, thereupon, to remind him that men have grown rich, as a rule, not by doing what thousands of others are doing but by undertaking something new. If instead of going into the retail dispensing of drugs, he had conceived and carried out the idea of the chain-drug store, he would have become an independently rich man.

There is always a chance to do this because the large majority of people do not think and, therefore, leave the field wide open for those who have something new with which to please the public. Negroes even found this possible during the days of slavery when the race supposedly had no chance at all.

About a hundred years ago Thomas Day, a North Carolina Negro, realized that the rough furniture of the people in his community did not meet the requirements of those of modern taste. He, therefore, worked out a style of ornate and beautiful furniture which attracted the attention of the most aristocratic people of the state and built up for himself a most successful business. Persons in that state are still talking about the Day

furniture, and not long ago it became the subject of a maga-
zine article. If North Carolina would turn out more Negroes
of this type today, instead of the rather large number who are
going to teach and preach, some of its present economic problems might thereby be solved.

During these same years another Negro was showing himself to be equally ingenious. This was Henry Boyd. After buying himself in Kentucky, he went to Cincinnati to start life as a
free man. There he encountered so much prejudice against
Negro labor that he could not find employment at his trade of
cabinetmaking. A new thought came to him, however; and in
this way he solved his own problem.

Boyd became convinced that people had been sleeping long
enough on straw ticks and wooden slats, and he invented the
corded bed, the most comfortable bed prior to the use of
springs which brought still more ease. Boyd's corded bed became popular throughout the Ohio and Mississippi Valleys,
and he built up a profitable trade which required the employment of twenty-five white and black artisans. Other enterprising Negro business men like Boyd gave the Negro element of
Cincinnati more of an aspect of progress before the Civil War
than it has today. Has the Negro less chance today than he
had a century ago?

For about thirty years the author knew an old Negro lady at
Gordonsville, Virginia, who gave the world something new in
frying chicken. She discovered the art of doing this thing in the
way that others could not, and she made a good living selling
her exceptionally prepared chicken and fried puffs at the windows of the cars when the trains stopped at the station. Well-
to-do men and women of both races would leave the Pullman
train with its modern diner attached and go out and supply
themselves and their friends with this old lady's tastefully
made up lunches.

Another woman of color living in Columbia, Missouri, recently gave the world another new idea. She had learned cook-
ing, especially baking, but saw no exceptional opportunity in
the usual application of the trade. After studying her situation
and the environment in which she had to live, she hit upon the

scheme of popularizing her savorous sweet potato biscuits, beaten whiter than all others by an invention of her own; and the people of both races made a well-beaten path to her home to enjoy these delicious biscuits. In this way she has made herself and her relatives independent.

This is the way fortunes are made, but Negroes, who are conscientiously doing their best to rise in the economic sphere, do not follow the noble examples of those who had less opportunity than we have today. We spend much time in slavish imitation, but our white friends strike out along new lines. Almost all of the large fortunes in America have been made in this way.

John D. Rockefeller did not set out in life to imitate Vanderbilt. Rockefeller saw his opportunity in developing the oil industry. Carnegie had better sense than to imitate Rockefeller, for that task was already well done, and he consolidated the steel interests. Henry Ford knew better than to take up what Carnegie had exploited, for there appeared a still larger possibility for industrial achievement in giving the world the facility of cheap transportation in the low-priced car.

While such guidance as the Negro needs will concern itself first with material things, however, it must not stop with these as ends in themselves. In the acquisition of these we lay the foundation for the greater things of the spirit. A poor man properly directed can write a more beautiful poem than one who is surfeited. The man in the hovel composes a more charming song than the one in the palace. The painter in the ghetto gets an inspiration for a more striking portrait than his landlord can appreciate. The ill-fed sculptor lives more abundantly than the millionaire who purchases the expression of his thought in marble and bronze. For the Negro, then, the door of opportunity is wide open. Let him prepare himself to enter this field where competition is no handicap. In such a sphere he may learn to lead the world, while keeping pace with it in the development of the material things of life.

CHAPTER XVI

THE NEW TYPE OF PROFESSIONAL MAN REQUIRED

Negroes should study for the professions for all sane reasons that members of another race should go into these lines of endeavor and also on account of the particular call to serve the lowly of their race. In the case of the law we should cease to make exceptions because of the possibilities for failure resulting from prejudice against the Negro lawyer and the lack of Negro business enterprises to require his services. Negroes must become like English gentlemen who study the law of the land, not because they intend to practice the profession, but because every gentleman should know the law. In the interpretation of the law by the courts, too, all the rights of the Negroes in this country are involved; and a larger number of us must qualify for this important service. We may have too many lawyers of the wrong kind, but we have not our share of the right kind.

The Negro lawyer has tended to follow in the footsteps of the average white practitioner and has not developed the power which he could acquire if he knew more about the people whom he should serve and the problems they have to confront. These things are not law in themselves, but they determine largely whether or not the Negro will practice law and the success he will have in the profession. The failure to give attention to these things has often meant the downfall of many a Negro lawyer.

There are, moreover, certain aspects of law to which the white man would hardly address himself but to which the Negro should direct special attention. Of unusual importance to the Negro is the necessity for understanding the misrepresentations in criminal records of Negroes, and race distinctions in the laws of modern nations. These matters require a systematic study of the principles of law and legal procedure and, in addition thereto, further study of legal problems as they meet the Negro lawyer in the life which he must live. This offers the Negro law school an unusual opportunity.

Because our lawyers do not give attention to these problems they often fail in a crisis. They are interested in the race and want to defend its cause. The case, however, requires not only the unselfish spirit they sometimes manifest but much more understanding of the legal principles involved. Nothing illustrates this better than the failure of one of our attorneys to measure up in the case brought up to the United States Supreme Court from Oklahoma to test the validity of the exclusion of Negroes from Pullman cars. The same criticism may be made of the segregation case of the District of Columbia brought before this highest tribunal by another Negro attorney. In both of these cases the lawyers started wrong and therefore ended wrong. They lacked the knowledge to present their cases properly to the court.

Our lawyers must learn that the judges are not attorneys themselves, for they have to decide on the merits of what is presented to them. It is not the business of the judges to amend their pleadings or decide their cases according to their good intentions. Certainly such generosity cannot be expected from prejudiced courts which are looking for every loophole possible to escape from a frank decision on the rights of Negroes guaranteed by the constitution. These matters require advanced study and painstaking research; but our lawyers, as a rule, are not interested in this sort of mental exercise.

The Negro medical schools have had a much better opportunity than the few Negro law schools which have functioned in the professional preparation of Negroes. On account of the racial contact required of white physicians who are sometimes unwilling to sustain this relation to Negroes the Negro physicians and dentists have a better chance among their people than the Negro lawyers; and the demand for the services of the former assures a larger income than Negro lawyers are accustomed to earn. But in spite of this better opportunity Negro medical institutions and their graduates have done little more than others to solve the peculiar problems confronting the Negro race.

Too many Negroes go into medicine and dentistry merely for selfish purposes, hoping thereby to increase their income and spend it in joyous living. They have the ambition to own fine automobiles, to dress handsomely, and to figure conspicuously in society. The practice of these professions among poor Negroes yields these results. Why not be a physician or dentist then?

Too many of our physicians are like the one whom the author recently visited in New York City. "When I heard you coming up the stairs," said he, "I began to feel glad, for I was sure that you were another patient from whom I might extract at least two dollars for a prescription."

Yet one would wonder how that physician could prosper in his profession, for he had no special equipment for the practice of any kind of advanced phases of medicine. About all he could do was to look at the patient's tongue, feel his pulse, ask him a few questions, write a prescription and collect the fee. The apparatus required for the modern treatment of serious maladies he did not have and seemed to have no ambition to possess.

The Negroes of today are very much in need of physicians who in their professional work will live up to what they are taught in school, and will build upon their foundation by both experience and further training. In his segregated position in the ghetto the Negro health problem presents more difficulties than that of the whites who are otherwise circumstanced. The longevity of the Negro depends in part upon the supply of Negro physicians and nurses who will address themselves unselfishly to the solution of this particular problem. Since the Negroes are forced into undesirable situations and compelled to inhabit germ-infested districts, they cannot escape ultimate extermination if our physicians do not help them to work out a community health program which will provide for the Negroes some way to survive.

Negro medical schools and their graduates must do more preaching of the necessity for improving conditions which determine health and eradicate disease. A large number of physicians and nurses must be trained, and new opportunities for them to practice must be found. This can be done by turning out better products from these schools and the extension of hospitals among Negroes who have been so long neglected. In this campaign, however, the Negro physicians must supply the leadership, and others must join with them in these efforts.

From medical schools, too, we must have Negroes with a program of medical research. Today the world is inclined to give attention to the health of the Negro since unsanitary conditions of the race will mean the loss of health among the whites. Philanthropists, however, hardly know how to proceed or which way to go because they have so long neglected the Negroes that they do not know how to provide wisely for them; and the Negro physicians themselves have failed to give adequate attention to these conditions. Negro medical students have not directed sufficient attention to the antebellum background of the Negro who, still under that influence, indulges in superstitious and religious practices which impede the progress of medicine among them. One would be surprised to know the extent to which primitive medicine is practiced among American Negroes today. Often in the rural districts they seldom see a physician. The midwife and the herb doctor there control the situation.

The greatest problem now awaiting solution is the investigation of the differential resistance of races to disease. What are the diseases of which Negroes are more susceptible than whites? What are the diseases of which the whites are more susceptible than Negroes? The Negro escapes yellow fever and influenza, but the white man dies. The white man withstands syphilis and tuberculosis fairly well, but the Negro afflicted with these maladies easily succumbs. These questions offer an inviting field of research for Negro medical students.

While we hear much about medicine, law and the like their importance must not be unduly emphasized. Certainly men should not crowd into these spheres to make money, but all professions among Negroes except those of teaching and preaching are undermanned. All Negroes in professions constitute less than two and a half percent of those over ten years of age who are gainfully employed. At the same time the whites find certain of their professions overcrowded, and some of their practitioners could not exist without the patronage of Negroes.

Negroes, too, should undergo systematic training for those professions in which they have shown special aptitude as in the arts. They must not wait for the Americans to approve their plunging into unknown spheres. The world is not circumscribed by the United States, and the Negro must become a pioneer in making use of a larger portion of the universe. If the people here do recognize the Negro in these spheres let him seek a hearing in the liberal circles of Europe. If he has any art Europeans will appreciate it and assure him success in forbidden fields.

In Europe, it should be noted, the Negro artist is not wanted as a mere imitator. Europeans will recognize him in the role of an enlightened artist portraying the life of his people. As an English abolitionist said more than a century ago, "The portrait of the Negro has seldom been drawn but by the pencil of his oppressor and the Negro has sat for it in the distorted attitude of slavery." A new method of approach, however, is now possible. There has been an awakening in Europe to the realization of the significance of African culture, and circles there want to see that life depicted by the Negro who can view it from within. There is a philosophy in it that the world must understand. From its contemplation may come a new social program. Herein lies the opportunity of the Negro artist as a world reformer. Will he see it and live or continue the mere imitation of others and die?

CHAPTER XVII

HIGHER STRIVINGS IN THE SERVICE OF THE COUNTRY

Another factor the Negro needs is a new figure in politics, one who will not concern himself so much with what others can do for him as with what he can do for himself. He will know sufficient about the system of government not to carry his trouble to the federal functionaries and thus confess himself a failure in the community in which he lives. He will know that his freedom from peonage and lynching will be determined by the extent that he can develop into a worthy citizen and impress himself upon his community.

The New Negro in politics will not be so unwise as to join the ignorant delegations from conferences and conventions which stage annual pilgrimages to the White House to complain to the President because they have socially and economically failed to measure up to demands of self-preservation. The New Negro in politics will understand clearly that in the final analysis federal functionaries cannot do anything about these matters within the police powers of the states, and he will not put himself in the position of being received with coldness and treated with contempt as these ignorant misleaders of the Negro race have been from time immemorial. The New Negro in politics, then, will appeal to his own and to such friends of other races in his locality as believe in social justice. If he does something for himself others will do more for him.

The increasing vigor of the race, then, will not be frittered away in partisan strife in the interest of the oppressors of the race. It ought not to be possible for the political bosses to induce almost any Negro in the community to abandon his permanent employment to assist them and their ilk in carrying out some program for the selfish purposes of the ones engineering the scheme. It ought not to be possible for the politicians to distribute funds at the rate of fifty or a hundred dollars a head among the outstanding ministers and use them and their congregations in vicious partisan strife. It is most shameful that some ministers resort to religion as a camouflage to gain influence in the churches only to use such power for selfish political purpose.

The Negro should endeavor to be a figure in politics, not a tool for the politicians. This higher role can be played not by parking all of the votes of a race on one side of the fence as both blacks and whites have done in the South, but by independent action. The Negro should not censure the Republican party for forgetting him and he should not blame the Democratic party for opposing him. Neither can the South blame any one but itself for its isolation in national politics. Any people who will vote the same way for three generations without thereby obtaining results ought to be ignored and disfranchised.

As a minority element the Negro should not knock at the door of any particular political party. He should appeal to the Negroes themselves and from them should come harmony and concerted action for a new advance to that larger freedom of men. The Negro should use his vote rather than give it away to reward the dead for some favors done in the distant past. He should clamor not for the few offices earmarked as Negro jobs but for the recognition of these despised persons as men according to the provision of the Constitution of the United States.

The few state and national offices formerly set aside for Negroes have paled into insignificance when compared with the many highly lucrative positions now occupied by Negroes as a result of their development in other spheres. Sometimes a Negro prominent in education, business or professional life can earn more in a few months than the most successful politicians can earn in years. These political jobs, moreover, have

diminished in recent years because the increase of race prejudice, which this policy has doubtless aided, supplies the
political leaders with an excuse for not granting their Negro
co-workers anything additional.

The New Negro in politics must learn something that the
old "ward-heelers" have never been able to realize, namely,
not only that the few offices allotted Negroes are insignificant
but that even if the Negro received a proportionate share of
the spoils, the race cannot hope to solve any serious problem
by the changing fortunes of politics. Real politics, the science
of government, is deeply rooted in the economic foundation of
the social order. To figure greatly in politics the Negro must be
a great figure in politics. A class of people slightly lifted above
poverty, therefore, can never have much influence in political
circles. The Negro must develop character and worth to make
him a desirable everywhere so that he will not have to knock
at the doors of political parties but will have them thrown
open to him.

The New Negro in politics must not ask the party for money,
he must not hire himself for a pittance to swing voters in line.
He must contribute to the campaign of the party pleasing him,
rather than draw upon it for an allowance to drive the wolf
from the door during the three months of the political can-
vass. It will be considered a stroke of good fortune that a
Negro of such influence and character has aligned himself
with a party, and this fact will speak eloquently for the element to which he belongs.

The New Negro in politics, moreover, must not be a politician. He must be a man. He must try to give the world something rather than extract something from it. The world, as he
should see it, does not owe him anything, certainly not a political office; and he should not try solely to secure one, and
thus waste valuable years which might be devoted to the development of something of an enduring value. If he goes into office, it should be as a sacrifice, because his valuable time is
required elsewhere. If he is needed by his country in a civil position, he may respond to the call as a matter of duty, for his
usefulness is otherwise assured. From such a Negro, then, we

may expect sound advice, intelligent guidance, and constructive effort for the good of all elements of our population.

When such Negroes go into office you will not find them specializing in things which peculiarly concern the Negroes, offering merely anti-lynching bills and measures for pensioning the freedmen. The New Negro in politics will see his opportunity not in thus restricting himself but in visioning the whole social and economic order with his race as a part of it. In thus working for the benefit of all as prompted by his liberal mindedness the New Negro will do much more to bring the elements together for common good than he will be able to do in prating only of the ills of his particular corner and extending his hand for a *douceur*.

In suggesting herein the rise of the New Negro in politics the author does not have in mind the so-called radical Negroes who have read and misunderstood Karl Marx and his disciples and would solve the political as well as the economic problems of the race by an immediate application of these principles. History shows that although large numbers of people have actually tried to realize such pleasant dreams, they have in the final analysis come back to a social program based on competition. If no one is to enjoy the fruits of his exceptional labor any more than the individual who is not prepared to render such extraordinary service, not one of a thousand will be sufficiently humanitarian to bestir himself to achieve much of importance, and force applied in this case to stimulate such action has always broken down. If the excited whites who are bringing to the Negroes such strange doctrines are insane enough to believe them, the Negroes themselves should learn to think before it is too late.

History shows that it does not matter who is in power or what revolutionary forces take over the government, those who have not learned to do for themselves and have to depend solely on others never obtain any more rights or privileges in the end than they had in the beginning. Even if the expected social upheaval comes, the Negro will be better prepared to take care of himself in the subsequent reconstruction if he develops the power to ascend to a position higher up after the radically democratic people will have recovered from their revelry in an impossible Utopia.

To say that the Negro cannot develop sufficiently in the business world to measure arms with present-day capitalists is to deny actual facts, refute history, and discredit the Negro as a capable competitor in the economic battle of life. No man knows what he can do until he tries. The Negro race has never tried to do very much for itself. The race has great possibilities. Properly awakened, the Negro can do the so-called impossible in the business world and thus help to govern rather than merely be governed.

In the failure to see this and the advocacy of the destruction of the whole economic order to right social wrong we see again the tendency of the Negro to look to some force from without to do for him what he must learn to do for himself. The Negro needs to become radical, and the race will never amount to anything until it does become so, but this radicalism should come from within. The Negro will be very foolish to resort to extreme measures in behalf of foreign movements before he learns to suffer and die to right his own wrongs. There is no movement in the world working especially for the Negro. He must learn to do this for himself or be exterminated just as the American Indian has faced his doom in the setting sun.

Why should the Negro wait for some one from without to urge him to self-assertion when he sees himself robbed by his employer, defrauded by his merchant, and hushed up by government agents of injustice? Why wait for a spur to action when he finds his manhood insulted, his women outraged, and his fellow men lynched for amusement? The Negroes have always had sufficient reason for being radical, and it looks silly to see them taking up the cause of others who pretend that they are interested in the Negro when they merely mean to use the race as a means to an end. When the desired purpose of these so-called friendly groups will have been served, they will have no further use for the Negro and will drop him just as the Republican machine has done.

The radicals bring forward, too, the argument that the Negro, being of a minority group, will always be overpowered by others. From the point of view of the selfish elements this may be true, and certainly it has worked thus for some time; but things do not always turn out according to mathematical calculations. In fact, the significant developments in history have never been thus determined. Only the temporary and the trivial can be thus forecast. The human factor is always difficult for the materialist to evaluate and the prophecies of the alarmist are often upset. Why should we expect less in the case of the Negro?

CHAPTER XVIII

THE STUDY OF THE NEGRO

The facts drawn from an experience of more than twenty years enable us to make certain deductions with respect to the study of the Negro. Only one Negro out of every ten thousand is interested in the effort to set forth what his race has thought and felt and attempted and accomplished that it may not become a negligible factor in the thought of the world. By traditions and education, however, the large majority of Negroes have become interested in the history and status of other races, and they spend millions annually to promote such knowledge. Along with this sum, of course, should be considered the large amount paid for devices in trying not to be Negroes.

The chief reason why so many give such a little attention to the background of the Negro is the belief that this study is unimportant. They consider as history only such deeds as those of Mussolini who after building up an efficient war machine with the aid of other Europeans would now use it to murder unarmed and defenseless Africans who have restricted themselves exclusively to attending to their own business. If Mussolini succeeds in crushing Abyssinia[1] he will be recorded in "history" among the Caesars, and volumes written in praise of the conqueror will find their way to the homes and libraries of thousands of mis-educated Negroes. The oppressor has always indoctrinated the weak with this interpretation of the crimes of the strong.

The war lords have done good only accidentally or incidentally while seeking to do evil. The movements which have ameliorated the condition of humanity and stimulated progress have been inaugurated by men of thought in lifting their fellows out of drudgery unto ease and comfort, out of selfishness unto altruism. The Negro may well rejoice that his hands, unlike those of his oppressors, are not stained with so much blood extracted by brute force. Real history is not the record of the successes and disappointments, the vices, the follies, and the quarrels of those who engage in contention for power.

The Association for the Study of Negro Life and History[2] is projected on the fact that there is nothing in the past of the Negro more shameful than what is found in the past of other races. The Negro is as human as the other members of the family of mankind. The Negro, like others, has been up at times; and at times he has been down. With the domestication of animals, the discovery of iron, the development of stringed instruments, an advancement in fine art, and the inauguration of trial by jury to his credit, the Negro stands just as high as others in contributing to the progress of the world.

The oppressor, however, raises his voice to the contrary. He teaches the Negro that he has no worthwhile past, that his race has done nothing significant since the beginning of time, and that there is no evidence that he will ever achieve anything great. The education of the Negro then must be carefully directed lest the race may waste time trying to do the impossible. Lead the Negro to believe this and thus control his thinking. If you can thereby determine what he will think, you will not need to worry about what he will do. You will not have to tell him to go to the back door. He will go without being told; and if there is no back door he will have one cut for his special benefit.

If you teach the Negro that he has accomplished as much good as any other race he will aspire to equality and justice without regard to race. Such an effort would upset the program of the oppressor in Africa and America. Play up before the Negro, then, his crimes and shortcomings. Let him learn to admire the Hebrew, the Greek, the Latin and the Teuton. Lead the Negro to detest the man of African blood—to hate himself. The oppressor then may conquer exploit, oppress and even annihilate the Negro by segregation without fear or trembling. With the truth hidden there will be little expression of thought to the contrary.

The American Negro has taken over an abundance of information which others have made accessible to the oppressed, but he has not yet learned to think and plan for himself as others do for themselves. Well might this race be referred to as the most docile and tractable people on earth. This merely means that when the oppressors once start the large majority of the race in the direction of serving the purposes of their traducers, the task becomes so easy in the years following that they have little trouble with the masses thus controlled. It is a most satisfactory system, and it has become so popular that European nations of foresight are sending some of their brightest minds to the United States to observe the Negro in "inaction" in order to learn how to deal likewise with Negroes in their colonies. What the Negro in America has become satisfied with will be accepted as the measure of what should be allotted him elsewhere. Certain Europeans consider the "solution of the race problem in the United States" one of our great achievements.

The mis-educated Negro joins the opposition with the objection that the study of the Negro keeps alive questions which should be forgotten. The Negro should cease to remember that he was once held a slave, that he has been oppressed, and even that he is a Negro. The traducer, however, keeps before the public such aspects of this history as will justify the present oppression of the race. It would seem, then, that the Negro should emphasize at the same time the favorable aspects to justify action in his behalf. One cannot blame the Negro for not desiring to be reminded of being the sort of creature that the oppressor has represented the Negro to be; but this very attitude shows ignorance of the past and a slavish dependence upon the enemy to serve those whom he would destroy. The Negro can be made proud of his past only by approaching it scientifically himself and giving his own story to the world. What others have written about the Negro during the last three centuries has been mainly for the purpose of bringing him where he is today and holding him there.

The method employed by the Association for the Study of Negro Life and History, however, is not spectacular propaganda or fire-eating agitation. Nothing can be accomplished in such fashion. "Whom the gods would destroy they first make mad." The Negro, whether in Africa or America, must be directed toward a serious examination of the fundamentals of education, religion, literature, and philosophy as they have been expounded to him. He must be sufficiently enlightened to determine for himself whether these forces have come into his life to bless him or to bless his oppressor. After learning the facts in the case the Negro must develop the power of execution to deal with these matters as do people of vision. Problems of great importance cannot be worked out in a day. Questions of great moment must be met with far-reaching plans.

The Association for the Study of Negro Life and History is teaching the Negro to exercise foresight rather than "hindsight." Liberia must not wait until she is offered to Germany before realizing that she has few friends in Europe. Abyssinia must not wait until she is invaded by Italy before she prepares for self-defense. A scientific study of the past of modern nations would show these selfish tendencies as inevitable results from their policies in dealing with those whom they have professed to elevate. For example, much of Africa has been conquered and subjugated to save souls. How expensive has been the Negro's salvation! One of the strong arguments for slavery was that it brought the Negro into the light of salvation. And yet the Negro today is all but lost.

The Association for the Study of Negro Life and History, however, has no special brand for the solution of the race problem except to learn to think. No general program of uplift for the Negroes in all parts of the world will be any more successful than such a procedure would be in the case of members of other races under different circumstances. What will help a Negro in Alabama may prove harmful to one in Maine. The African Negro may find his progress retarded by applying "methods used for the elevation of the Negro in America." A thinking man, however, learns to deal wisely with conditions as he finds them rather than to take orders from some one who knows nothing about his status and cares less. At present the Negro, both in Africa and America, is being turned first here and there experimentally by so-called friends who in the final analysis assist the Negro merely in remaining in the dark.

In the furtherance of the program of taking up these matters dispassionately the Association had made available an outline for the systematic study of the Negro as he has touched the life of others and as others have functioned in their relation to him, *The African Background Outlined: A Handbook*. This book is written from the point of view of history, literature, art, education, religion and economic imperialism. In seventeen chapters as Part I of the work a brief summary of the past in Africa is presented; and courses on "The Negro in Africa," "The Negro in the European Mind," "The Negro in America," "The Negro in Literature," "The Negro in Art," "The Education of the Negro," "The Religious Development of the Negro," and "Economic Imperialism," follow as Part II with ample bibliographical comment for every heading and subhead of these outlines. This facilitates the task of clubs, young peoples' societies, and special classes organized where the oppressors of the race and the Negroes cooperating with them are determined that the history and status of the Negro shall not be made a part of the curricula.

In this outline there is no animus, nothing to engender race hate. The Association does not bring out such publications. The aim of this organization is to set forth facts in scientific form, for facts properly set forth will tell their own story. No advantage can be gained by merely inflaming the Negro's mind against his traducers. In a manner they deserve to be congratulated for taking care of their own interests so well. The Negro needs to become angry with himself because he has not handled his own affairs wisely. In other words, the Negro must learn from others how to take care of himself in this trying ordeal. He must not remain content with taking over what others set aside for him and then come in the guise of friends to subject even that limited information to further misinterpretation.

APPENDIX

MUCH ADO ABOUT A NAME

A participant who recently attended an historical meeting desired to take up the question as to what the race should be called. *Africans, Negroes, colored people*, or what? This is a matter of much concern to him because he hopes thereby to solve the race problem. If others will agree to call Negroes Nordics, he thinks, he will reach the desired end by taking a short cut.

This may sound all but insane, but there are a good many "highly educated" Negroes who believe that such can be accomplished by this shift in terminology; and they have spent time and energy in trying to effect a change. Many of this class suffer mentally because of the frequent use of "offensive expressions" in addressing Negroes. When dealing with them, then, one has to be very careful. For this reason our friends in other races have to seek guidance in approaching us. For example, Lady Simon, the wife of Sir John Simon of the British Cabinet, has recently asked an American Negro what his people prefer to be called; and later in England she took up the same matter with another member of this race. Being an advocate of freedom, she has written considerably to advance its cause. She would not like to use in her works, then, an expression which may hurt some one's feelings.

Although a student of social problems, this learned woman cannot fathom this peculiar psychology. Americans, too, must confess the difficulty of understanding it, unless it is that the "highly educated Negro mind" tends to concern itself with trifles rather than with the great problems of life. We have known

Negroes to ask for a separate Y.M.C.A. or Y.W.C.A., a separate church or a separate school, and then object to calling the institution *colored* or *Negro*. These segregationists have compromised on principle, but they are unwilling to acknowledge their crime against justice. The name, they believe, will save them from the disgrace.

It does not matter so much what the thing is called as what the thing is. The Negro would not cease to be what he is by calling him something else; but, if he will struggle and make something of himself and contribute to modern culture, the world will learn to look upon him as an American rather than as one of an undeveloped element of the population.

The word *Negro* or *black* is used in referring to this particular element because most persons of native African descent approach this color. The term does not imply that every Negro is black; and the word white does not mean that every white man is actually white. Negroes may be *colored*, but many Caucasians are scientifically classified as *colored*. We are not all Africans, moreover, because many of us were not born in Africa; and we are not all Afro-Americans, because few of us are natives of Africa transplanted to America.

There is nothing to be gained by running away from the name. The names of practically all races and nations at times have connoted insignificance and low social status. Angles and Saxons, once the slaves of Romans, experienced this; and even the name of the Greek for a while meant no more than this to these conquerors of the world. The people who bore these names, however, have made them grand and illustrious. The Negro must learn to do the same.

It is strange, too, that while the Negro feels ashamed of his name, persons abroad do not usually think of it in this sense. One does find in Europe a number of West Indian and American Negroes of some Caucasian blood, who do not want to be known as Negroes. As a rule, however, a European of African Negro blood feels proud of this racial heritage and delights to be referred to as such. The writer saw a striking case of this in London in the granddaughter of a Zulu chief. She is so far removed from the African type that one could easily mistake her for a Spaniard; and yet she thinks only for her African connection and gets her inspiration mainly from the story of her people beyond the Pillars of Hercules.

The writer was agreeably surprised a few days later, too, when he met a prominent Parisian with the same attitude. He has produced several volumes in which he champions the cause of the Negro because he has in his veins the same blood. A well-to-do European woman, the daughter of a Dutchman and an African mother, is similarly enthusiastic over her Negro blood. The first thing she mentioned in conversing with the writer was that black mother. This young woman expressed the regret that she did not have more of that color that she, too, might say, as do members of certain tribes of Africa: "I am black and comely. I am black and beautiful. I am beautifully black."

These people surprise you when you think of the attitude of many American Negroes on this question. These race-conscious people can think, but it is seldom that the American Negro indulges in such an exercise. He has permitted other people to determine for him the attitude that he has toward his own people. This means the enslavement of his mind and eventually the enslavement of his body.

Some Europeans rather regard the word Negro as romantic. Going now along the streets of Paris, one will see advertised such places as "I 'Elan Noir," and the "Café au Nègre de Toulouse." In one of these cases the writer was especially attracted by the "Choppe du Nègre" and took dinner there one day. The cuisine was excellent, the music rendered by the orchestra was charming, and a jolly crowd came to enjoy themselves. However, he was the only "Nègre" there.

Walking along a street in Geneva not long ago, the writer's attention was attracted to something of the sort, which is still more significant. It was a wholesale coffee house called "A La Case de I'Oncle Tom." He entered and asked: "Why did you give this store such a name?" The proprietress laughed and explained that her grandfather, Francois Prudhom, who had read "Uncle Tom's Cabin" and had been deeply impressed thereby, selected this name for the store when he established it in 1866.

THE VALUE OF COLOR

Not long ago the writer saw on a street car one of the prettiest women in the world. She was a perfectly black woman becomingly dressed in suitable gray and modest adornments which harmonized with her color. She was naturally a commanding figure without any effort to please others, for her bearing was such that she would not fail to attract attention. He could not restrain himself from gazing at her; and, looking around to see whether others were similarly concerned, he found the whites in the car admiring her also, even to the point of commenting among themselves.

This woman's common sense, manifested in knowing how to dress, had made her color an asset rather than a liability. The writer easily recalled, then, that tribe in Africa that feels unusually proud of being black. We are told that they are so anxious to be black that if they find one of the group with a tendency to depart the least from this color they go to the heart of nature and extract from it its darkest dye and paint therewith that native's face that he may continue perfectly black.

Here in America, however, we are ashamed of being black. So many of us who are actually black powder our faces and make ourselves blue. In so doing we become all but hideous by the slavish aping of those around us in keeping with our custom of imitation. We fail to take ourselves for what we are actually worth, and do not make the most of ourselves.

We show lack of taste in the selection of our dress. We long for what others wear whether it harmonizes with our color or not. They have given particular attention to design with respect to their race and have written books to this effect. Thinking, however, that the Negro is not supposed to wear anything but what the poor may pick up, the artists have not thought seriously of him. Both teachers and students of nearby schools thus concerned, then, repeatedly appeal to us for help in the study of design with respect to the Negro, but we have nothing scientific to offer them. We have no staff of artists who can function in this sphere.

To be able to supply this need requires the most painstaking effort to understand colors and color schemes. It is a very difficult task because of the variation of color within the race. Sometimes in one family of ten you will hardly find two of the same shade. To dress them all alike may be economical, but the world thereby misses that much of beauty. The Negro mother, then, needs to be the real artist, and the schools now training the youth to be the parents of tomorrow should give as much attention to these things esthetic as they do to language, literature or mathematics.

In neglecting to know himself better from this point of view, then, the Negro is making a costly mistake. He should be deeply concerned with the esthetic possibilities of his situation. In this so-called Negro race we have the prettiest people in the world, when they dress in harmony with the many shades and colors with which we are so richly endowed. Why do we go away from home to find what we already have on hand?

Recently one saw in Washington a demonstration of the value of color when the Masonic conclave staged a tremendous parade in this national city. The whites were attracted to the upstanding, outstanding Negroes so becomingly bedecked in costumes of the Orient. This, however, was accidental. The color of the Negroes happened to be Oriental, and the colors of this order were originally worked out to suit the people of those parts. The dead white of the Caucasian does not harmonize with such garb. Why, then should the Negro worry about what others wear?

Carrying the imitation of others to an extreme today, we do not find ourselves far in advance of the oppressed antebellum Negroes, who, unable to dress themselves, had to take whatever others threw at them. We make a most hideous spectacle, then, when we are on dress parade in our social atmosphere. So many of us clad in unbecoming colors often look like decorated pet horses turned loose for an hour or so of freedom.

Appreciating the value of color, the artists in European cities are trying to change their hue to that of the colored people.

They can understand how inexpressive the dead white is, and they are trying to make use of what we are seeking to conceal. The models in their shops are purposely colored to display to good effect the beautiful costumes which require color. Some of these Europeans frankly tell Negroes how they envy them for their color.

One is not surprised, then, to find European cafés and hotels employing American or African Negroes to supply this color which the Europeans lack. Pictures of such black men are sometimes displayed to great effect. That of Josephine Baker adorns the windows of large stores in Paris. Here in America, too, we observe that art centers are likewise getting away from the dead white to enjoy the richness of color.

The writer felt somewhat encouraged recently when he talked with a Washington lady who runs "The Pandora," a unique establishment devoted to design. Upon inquiring about her progress in the effort to teach colored people how to wear what becomes them, she reported considerable success. Sometimes customers insist on purchasing unbecoming attire, but usually she has shown them the unwisdom of so doing, and most of them now take her advice.

In this way this enterprising woman is not only conducting a pioneer business, but she is rendering a social service. She has not had any special training in this work, but on her initiative she is building upon what she has learned by studying the Negroes in her community. Others of us may do likewise, if we try to help the Negro rather than exploit him.

Appendix

SELECTED LETTERS AND ARTICLES BY CARTER G. WOODSON

A LETTER TO W. E. B. DU BOIS

Carter G. Woodson to W. E. B. Du Bois, February 18, 1908, MS 312, W. E. B. Du Bois Papers, Special Collections and University Archives, University of Massachusetts Amherst Libraries

In this letter, Woodson expressed interest in studying the history of the African American church for his master's thesis and appeals to Du Bois for research support, likely because he could not find guidance from the faculty at the University of Chicago. The letter reveals Woodson's early interest in studying black history and culture, though he would not be able to formally do so until after he completed doctoral studies at Harvard University.

> Chicago, Ill. Feb 18, 1908
> Prof. W. B. DuBois, Ph.D.,
> Atlanta, Ga.

Dear Sir:

I have the honor to say that I was a Negro student of the University of Chicago where I hope to appear in June for examination as a candidate for its degree of Master of Arts. The subject of my thesis is the <u>Negro Church</u>.

Knowing that for a long time you have studied the different institutions of the race, I believe that you can give me much information on this subject. Surely you are in position to tell me where such information may be found. Whatever you may be able to do to help me will be most gratefully acknowledged, and any expense?? in so doing will be born by him who reluctantly asks for so much of your valuable time.

It should be stated, also, that I am anxious to get statistics as to the number of churches in each state, their wealth, membership, intellectual status, and general aspects; in short all such facts as will show what the church has contributed to the <u>progress</u> or <u>regress</u> of the race.

Begging your indulgence for this bold request I subscribe myself.

> Yours very respectfully,
> C. G. Woodson,
> Room 107 Middle Divinity Hall,
> University of Chicago,
> Chicago, Ill.

LETTERS TO JESSE E. MOORLAND

Carter G. Woodson to Jesse E. Moorland, May 15, 1920 & May 22, 1920, Box 126-34, Folder 695, Jesse E. Moorland Papers, Moorland-Spingarn Research Center, Howard University

Woodson expressed his frustration with Howard University's white president, J. Stanley Durkee, to Moorland, a prominent black minister who donated his extensive collection of books on black life to Howard University, establishing the foundation of its research library. In this letter, Woodson also accused Moorland of being too accommodating of white liberals, even when their policies and leadership undermined the objectives of black education.

Correspondence between
Carter G. Woodson and Jesse E. Moorland

CONFIDENTIAL

May 15, 1920

> Dr. J. E. Moorland,
> 347 Madison Ave.,
> New York City, N.Y.

My dear Dr. Moorland:

I have just read your personal letter to me. You seem
to misunderstand or evade the question. The question is
this: In as much as Northern teachers of the missionary
spirit no longer come South to work among Negroes and
those now coming for this purpose are less qualified in
their fields than the average Negro teacher, will you
permit such inefficient white leadership to bludgeon well
educated Negro instructors among them into submission
to their mediaeval methods thrown aside centuries ago
by white educators. In other words, do you stand for the
Negro race or for the whites? This is the question which
you as well as every other Negro in a position of
leadership must now answer. I sincerely hope that you
will be loyal to your people. They have been trodden
under foot long enough and I do not like to see any
Negro trying to defend their oppressors.

The fact is this: Durkee has treated several other
teachers at Howard University much worse than he has
treated me. I react and they do not. Some of them have
not enough manhood and others are afraid of losing
their jobs. He is so uneducated that he can not properly
use the English language. I have had to write a letter for
him myself because he does not know how to present a
proposition to a business man. He has to take advice
from almost everybody and, not knowing anything
about education, he acts on conflicting advice which
keeps him in a muddle and the school in an uproar. He is
not a Christian except in form, for he acts on rumors

without investigation and condemns a man without giving him a hearing. In fact, he is a swaggerer, always bragging about what he is going to do before he does it, and he usually fails to do what he says God has told him that He will enable him to do.

Durkee has only one gift and that is an utterly worthless one in education. He can dramatize an idea taken from poetry of the Bible, but he never has an original idea. Having studied oratory and elocution a number of years, he can for a while easily sway the masses. I am surprised, however, that men of your type have been so unwise as to impose upon Howard University such a slave driver to masquerade as an educator. Have you not had enough of slavery?

Your traditional premise to the effect that it is wise to unite the best of the two races is fundamentally wrong when this means the subjection of the best in the Negro race to the most inefficient of the white race. Your own judgment should lead you to realize that white men who are now teaching in Negro schools and administering their affairs are not the best of that race. You cannot be so stupid as to think such non-sense. Durkee himself is a case in evidence. When he came to Howard University he was boomed as a man of tremendous power and much contact with the rich. All of this is untrue. He has not as much contact with the rich as I have and cannot approach such people. In fact, he has no contact but what the school gives him. The funds recently obtained for the Medical School were secured by Scott through Julius Rosenwald. When Durkee approached the General Education Board they easily got rid of him with an excuse. He boasted of being sure to get $1,650,000 from Congress because it had been spoken to him out of the mouth of God, but he actually got about 9% of this amount. Should a bluffing slave driver of this type be permitted to ruin Howard University? Again I ask: Are you with the whites who are exploiting the Negroes or with those Negroes who still cry for deliverance from the oppressor?

                    Respectfully yours,
                    C.G. Woodson

If well educated Negroes cannot remain at Howard University without losing their self respect, what hope is there for the Negro youth? Well educated white men are not found in Negro schools because they can earn so much more in their own institutions; and even if they could earn the same, they would prefer their own because of the social proscription suffered in teaching Negroes. There is not in Howard University, including the President, a single white man who has made an impression in any field. There are at Howard, however, several Negroes whose scholarship is known at home and abroad. What is the propriety then in subjecting the philosopher of Athens to the barbarian of Sparta?

                    C.G.W.

A LYNCHING IN WASHINGTON, D.C.

Carter G. Woodson, "A Lynching in Washington, D.C.," *The Negro in Our History* (Associated Publishers, 1922), 326–28

Woodson described his experience witnessing a lynching during the Red Summer of 1919 in the first textbook he published. It is worth noting that Woodson references lynching multiple times in *The Mis-education of the Negro*.

On the nineteenth of July, 1919, then, there appeared in the streets of Washington, a number of soldiers, sailors and marines, who because of exaggerated reports that Negroes had assaulted white women and the rumor that the wife of a marine had been thus attacked, proceeded to the southwest section of Washington where they beat several innocent Negroes. On Sunday, the following day, these whites on leave from the United States Army and Navy, supported by civilians, had effected a better organization to carry out their purposes. They formed at Pennsylvania Avenue and Seventh Street a mob which took over the city from the Capitol to the White House. Negroes were pulled from vehicles and street cars and beaten into unconsciousness. One was thus taken possession of by the mob and beaten unmercifully right in front of the White House, where the President must have heard his groans but has not as yet uttered a word of protest. Other Negroes were shot and left to die on the streets.

Going along Pennsylvania Avenue, that night, the author himself walked into the midst of the mob at the intersection of Eighth Street and Pennsylvania Avenue. Before he realized where he was, there resounded shots all around him. A large mob swept down Pennsylvania Avenue pursuing a Negro yelling for mercy, while another mob at the debouchment of Eighth Street had caught a Negro whom they conveniently adjusted for execution and shot while the author, walking briskly as possible to escape the same fate himself, heard the harassing groans of the Negro. To be sure that their murderous task was well done a leader yelled to the executioners, "Did you get him?" The reply was, "Yes, we got him."

The events of the following day, however, showed that this mob had misjudged the Washington Negroes. They made extensive preparation for the retaliatory onslaught of the whites. Weapons were bought, houses were barricaded, and high powered automobiles were armored for touring the city late in the night. The augmented police force and the 300 provost guards supplied with rifles and machine guns did not deter the Negroes. When attacked by the white mob they easily stood their ground, and took the offensive when the white mob attempted to invade Negro quarters, although Thomas Armistead, charging in defense of the Negroes, fell mortally wounded. Whereas the whites wounded about 300 Negroes the Sunday night when they were not expecting the attack, the casualty list of Monday night showed two Negroes and four whites killed and a much larger number of whites wounded than Negroes.

A riot almost of the same order broke out in Chicago a few weeks later. In that city the large migration of Negroes to its industrial plants and the invasion of desirable residential districts by these newcomers incensed the whites to the point of precipitating a race war. The Negroes, however, showed by the number of whites killed the same tendency of the Washington Negro to retaliate when attacked by cowards. The Negro helped to save democracy abroad, but he must fight to enjoy it at home.

TWENTY YEARS WASTED, SAYS D.C. HISTORIAN

Carter G. Woodson, "Twenty Years Wasted, Says D.C. Historian," *Negro World*, March 21, 1931, 1, 8

Woodson explains how and why it took him twenty years to "recover" from his formal educational training at the most prestigious universities in the world.

"In a course, at Harvard, for example, we were required to find out whether Pericles was justly charged with trying to supplant the worship of Jupiter with that of Juno. Since that time I have learned that I would have been better prepared for work among the Negroes in the Black Belt if I had spent that time learning why John Jasper of sun-do-move fame joined with Joshua in contending that the planet stood still 'In the middle of the line while he fought the battle the second time.' It has taken me twenty years to recover from my education. How unfortunate it is for a man to waste no much valuable time. I thank God that the veil has been lifted at last, and I can now see the drama of life in which my people play such an uncourageous role.

"I would not close any Negro college of university, but I would reconstruct the whole system. I would not eliminate many of the courses now being offered, but I would secure men of vision to give them from the point of view of the people to be served. I would not spend the money for the higher education of the Negro, but I would redefine higher education as preparation to serve the lowly rather than to live as an aristocrat."

REVOLUTION MUST COME

"This revolution in our education must come. It may not be effected immediately; but it is inevitable, for its necessity is evident, even to a casual observer. Those Negros who have been trained the most serve the least. Negro preachers who are graduates of the best schools of theology preach to our smallest congregations. Our physicians and lawyers who have undergone training in leading universities of the land often have difficulty in making a living. Teachers of 'ripe scholarship' influence the youth less than those of limited training. Such maladjusted workers complain that since Negroes are ignorant, they prefer ignorant leadership, but the trouble is not that the people are ignorant but that these misfits are ignorant of the people.

"Some one has asked me what changes I would make in the curricula of Negro schools. Such subjects of certitude as mathematics, of course, would continue and so would most of the work in practical languages and science. In theology, literature, social science, and education, however, radical reconstruction is necessary. The old worn-out theories as to man's relation to God and his fellow man, the system of thought which has permitted one man to exploit, oppress and exterminate another and still be regarded as righteous must be discarded for the new thought of men as brethren and the idea of God as the lover of all man kind."

CUT OUT SHAKESPEARE

"After Negro students have mastered the fundamentals of English, the principles of composition, and the leading facts in the development of its literature, they should not spend all of their time in advanced work on Shakespeare, Chaucer and Anglo-Saxon. They should direct their attention to the folklore of the African, to the philosophy in the proverbs and other thought of Negroes, to the development of the Negro in the use of modern language and to the works of Negro writers."

STUDY AFRICAN BACKGROUND

"The leading facts of the history of the world should be studied by all, but of what advantage is it to the Negro student of history to devote all of his time to courses bearing on such despots as Alexander the Great, Caesar, and Napoleon, or to the record of those nations whose outstanding achievement, has been rapine, plunder, and murder for world power? Why not study the African background from the point of view of anthropology and history, and why not take up sociology, as it concerns the Negro peasant or proletarian who is suffering from sufficient ills, to supply laboratory work for the most advanced students of the social order? Why not take up economics as reflected by the Negroes of today and work out some remedy for their lack of capital, the absence of cooperative enterprise, and the short life of their establishments?"

THE MISEDUCATION OF THE NEGRO

Carter G. Woodson, "The Miseducation of the Negro," *The Crisis*, August 1931, 266–67

This article presents Woodson's early conceptualization of "mis-education," anticipating many of the central claims expounded upon in the book.

In their own as well as in mixed schools, Negroes are taught to admire the Hebrew, the Greek, the Latin, and the Teuton and to despise the African. The thought of the inferiority of the Negro is drilled into him in almost every class he enters. If he happens to leave school after he has mastered the fundamentals, before he has finished high school or reached college, he will naturally escape from some of this bias and may recover in time to be of service to his people.

Practically all of the successful Negroes in this country are those who never learned this prejudice "scientifically" because they entered upon their life's work without formal education. The large majority of the Negroes who have put on the finishing touches of our best colleges, however, are all but worthless in the uplift of their people. If, after leaving school, they have the opportunity to give out to Negroes what traducers of the race have taught them, such persons may earn a living by teaching or preaching to Negroes what someone would like to have them know, but they never become a constructive force in the elevation of those far down. They become estranged from the masses and the gap between them widens as the years go by.

The explanation of this is a simple problem. The schools and colleges of this country are so conducted as to produce this result. For example, an officer of a Negro university, thinking that an additional course on the Negro should be given there, called upon a Negro Doctor of Philosophy of the faculty to offer such work. He promptly informed the officer that he knew nothing about the Negro. He did not go to school to waste his time that way. He went to be educated.

Last year at one of the Negro summer schools, a white instructor gave a course on the Negro, using for his text a work of Jerome Dowd, who teaches that whites are superior to blacks. When asked by one of the students why he used such a textbook, the instructor replied that he wanted them to get Dowd's point of view. If schools for Negroes are places where they must be convinced of their inferiority, they cannot escape from their tormentors and rise to recognition and usefulness.

As another has well said, to handicap a student for life by

teaching him that his black face is a curse and that his struggle to change his condition is hopeless is the worst kind of lynching. It kills one's aspirations and dooms him to vagabondage and crime.

In most cases, moreover, when the teachers of Negroes are persons of good intentions, the result is the same. In the school of business administration, for example, Negroes are trained exclusively in the economics and psychology of Wall Street, and are thereby made to despise the opportunities to conduct laundries, repair shoes, run ice wagons, push banana carts, and sell peanuts among their own people. Foreigners, who have not studied economics and psychology but have studied Negroes, take up this business and grow rich while the "highly educated" Negroes are complaining because the native American whites do not permit the blacks to share what others have developed.

In schools of journalism Negroes are being taught how to edit such metropolitan dailies as the *Chicago Tribune* and the *New York Times*, which would hardly hire a Negro as a janitor; and when such graduates come to the Negro weeklies for employment they are not prepared to function in such establishments, which to be successful must be built upon accurate knowledge of the psychology and philosophy of the Negro.

In the schools of religion Negro ministers devote their time to dead languages and dead issues, to the dogma of other races, the schism produced by unnecessary disputes, and the conflicts by which fanatics have moistened the soil of Asia and Europe with the blood of unoffending people. These "highly educated" Negro ministers, then, know practically nothing of the religious background of their parishioners, do not appreciate their philosophy of life, and do not understand their spiritual development as influenced by African survivals in America and the peculiar development of the Negro church. The result, therefore, is that while the illiterate minister who has given attention to these things preaches to the masses, the "highly educated" Negro minister talks to benches.

The Negroes who have been trained the most serve the least. Our physicians and lawyers who have undergone training in the leading universities of the land often have difficulty in making a living. Teachers of "ripe scholarship" influence the youth less than those of limited training. Such mal-adjusted workers complain that, since Negroes are ignorant, they prefer ignorant leaders; but the trouble is not that the people are ignorant, but that these misfits are ignorant of the people.

Unfortunately these conditions have continued because schools for Negroes have always been established in mushroom fashion, without giving sufficient thought to the needs of the people to be thus served, and most of those now promoting Negro education are proceeding in the same way. Talking the other day with one of the men now giving millions to establish four Negro universities in the South, I find that he is of the opinion that you can go almost anywhere and build a three-million-dollar plant, place in charge a man to do what you want accomplished, and in a short while he can secure or have trained to order the men necessary to make a university.

Such a thing cannot be done because there are not sufficient Negroes or whites in this country qualified to conduct for Negroes such a university as they need. Most of the whites who are now serving Negroes as educators come to them as persons bearing gifts from a foreign shore, and the Negroes gather around them in childlike fashion, gazing with astonishment and excitement to find out what these things mean.

All things being equal, however, there should be no different method of approach or appeal to Negro students that cannot be made just as well by a white teacher to Negro students or a Negro teacher to white students, if such teachers are properly informed and have the human attitude; but tradition, race, hate, and terrorism have made such a thing impossible. However, I am not an advocate of segregation. I do not believe in separate schools. I am merely emphasizing the necessity for common-sense schools and teachers who understand and continue in sympathy with those whom they instruct.

Those who take the position to the contrary have the idea that education is merely a process of imparting information. One who can give out these things or devise an easy plan for so doing, then, is an educator. In a sense this is true, this machine method accounts for most of the troubles of the Negro. For me, education means to inspire people to live more abundantly, to learn to begin with life as they find it and make it better.

The instruction so far given in Negro Colleges and universities has worked to the contrary. In most cases such graduates have merely increased the number of malcontents who offer no program for changing the undesirable conditions about which they complain.

The seat of the trouble is in what Negroes are now being taught. Their education does not bring their minds into harmony with life as they must face it. When a Negro student works his way through college by shining shoes he does not think of making a special study of the science underlying the production and distribution of leather and its products, that he may some day figure in this sphere. The Negro boy sent to college by a mechanic seldom dreams of learning mechanical engineering to build upon the foundation his father has laid, that in years to come he may figure as a contractor or a consulting engineer. The Negro girl who goes to college hardly wants to return to her mother if she is a washerwoman, but this girl should come back with sufficient knowledge of physics and chemistry and business administration to use her mother's work as a nucleus for a modern steam laundry.

A white professor of a Southern university recently resigned his position to get rich by running a laundry for Negroes. A Negro college instructor would have considered such a suggestion an insult. The so-called education of Negro college graduates leads them to throw away opportunities which they have and go in quest of those which they do not find. A school system which thus handicaps people for life by setting them adrift is not worthy of public support.

In the case of the white youth in this country, they can choose their courses more at random and still succeed because of numerous opportunities offered by their people, but even they show so much more wisdom than do Negroes. For example, a year or two after I left Harvard I found out West a schoolmate who was studying wool. "How did you happen to get into this sort of thing," I inquired. His people, he replied, had had some experience in wool and in college he prepared himself for this work by studying its economic foundation. When I was at Harvard I studied Aristotle, Plato, Marsiglio of Padua, and Pascasius Rathbertus. My friend who studied wool, however, is now independently rich and has sufficient leisure to enjoy the cultural side of life which his knowledge of the science underlying his business developed, but I have to make my living by begging for a struggling cause.

From this indictment of our schools, then, one may conclude that it would serve the public better to keep Negroes away from them. Such an unwise course, however, is not herein suggested. The thing needed is reform. Negro institutions of learning and those of whites, too, especially those white institutions which are training teachers who have to deal with large numbers of Negroes, should reconstruct their curricula. These institutions should abandon a large portion of the traditional courses which have been retained throughout the years because they are supposedly cultural, and they should offer instead training in things which are also cultural and at the same time have a bearing on the life of the people thus taught. Certainly the Negro should learn something about the history and culture of the white man with whom he has to deal daily, and the white man should likewise learn the same about the Negro; but if the education of either is made a one-sided effort neither one will understand or appreciate the other, and interracial cooperation will be impossible.

Looking over the recent catalogues of the leading Negro colleges, I find their courses drawn up without much thought about the Negro. Invariably these institutions give courses in ancient, medieval, and modern Europe, but they do not offer courses in ancient, medieval, and modern Africa. Yet Africa, according to recent discoveries, has contributed about as much to the progress of mankind as Europe has, and the early civilization of the Mediterranean world was decidedly influenced by the so-called Dark Continent.

Negro colleges offer courses bearing on the European colonists prior to their coming to America, their settlement on these shores, and their development here toward independence. Why not be equally as generous with the Negroes in treating their status in Africa prior to enslavement, their first transplantation to the West Indies, the Latinization of certain Negroes in contradistinction to the development of others under the influence of the Teuton, and the effort of the race toward self expression in America?

A further examination of the curricula of Negro colleges shows, too, that as a rule they offer courses in Greek philosophy and in modern European thought, but direct no attention to the philosophy of the Negro. Negroes have and always have had their own ideas about purpose, change, time, and space, about appearance and reality, and about freedom and necessity. The effort of the Negro to interpret man's relation to the universe shows just as much intelligence as we find in the philosophy of the Greeks. There were many Africans who were just as wise as Socrates.

Again I find in some of these catalogues numerous courses in art, but no well defined course in Negro or African art. The art of Africa, however, influenced the art of the Greeks to the extent that thinkers are now saying that the most ancient culture of the Mediterranean was chiefly African. Most of these colleges, too, do not even direct special attention to Negro music in which the race has made an outstanding contribution in America.

The unreasonable attitude is that because the whites do not have these things in their schools the Negroes must not have them in theirs. The Catholics and Jews, therefore, are wrong in establishing special schools to teach the principles of their religion, and the Germans in the United States are unwise in having their children taught their mother tongue.

The higher education of the Negro, then, has been largely meaningless imitation. When the Negro finishes his course in one of our schools, he knows what others have done, but he has not been inspired to do much for himself. If he makes a success in life it comes largely by accident.

LETTERS TO BENJAMIN BRAWLEY

Carter G. Woodson to Benjamin Brawley,
November 27, 1931 & January 7, 1932,
W. E. B. Du Bois Papers (MS 312) Special
Collections and University Archives, University of
Massachusetts Amherst Libraries

In these letters to Howard University professor Benjamin
Brawley, Woodson explains his decision not to participate
in a convening called by the Phelps Stokes Fund to develop
an encyclopedia on the Negro. In doing so, Woodson outlines his critiques of white philanthropists' ongoing manipulation of black education and scholarship.

November 27, 1931

Professor Benjamin Brawley,
Howard University,
Washington, D.C.

My dear Professor Brawley:

I have the report of your conference on the advisability
of publishing an encyclopedia of the Negro, held in
Washington, D.C., November 7, 1931. I note that it was
voted that I attend the next meeting.

I consider it inadvisable for me to attend, however, for
the reason that the persons who called the meeting
evidently did not desire my cooperation. Furthermore, a
number of the persons attending could not have been
ignorant of the fact that since 1922 the Association for
the Study of Negro Life and History, in cooperation with
the Associated Publishers, has been collecting data for
such an encyclopedia and has actually begun the
editorial work.

I should add that our plan is to publish a work of ten
volumes, the title of which will be THE ENCYCLOPEDIA
AFRICANA. There can be no legal objection to your

duplicating our efforts, but we respectfully request that you use some other title.

I take this occasion to say, too, that inasmuch as this work is already in the making and you have not as yet definitely decided what you will do that you should spend your time and energy in doing some of the other long neglected tasks which the present undesirable condition of the Negro requires. There is so much to be done for the Negro that it sems to me to be unwise and unnecessary for one agency to duplicate the efforts of the other.

Respectfully yours,
C. G. Woodson,
Director.

January 7, 1932

Professor Benjamin Brawley,
1201 Harvard Street, N.W.,
Washington, D.C.

Dear Sir:

I have this day received the memorandum with respect to the conference on the advisability of publishing an Encyclopedia of the Negro. Inasmuch as I have already informed you in another communication that I shall not attend, it is not necessary for me to cover that ground in this letter. I desire now, however, to bring before you certain facts which should concern every one invited to this conference and every person interested in the uplift of the race.

This movement on the part of the Phelps Stokes Fund to produce a work embodying the history and present status of the Negro is an effort to duplicate and, if possible, to destroy the work of the Association for the Study of Negro Life and History, which, under my direction has not evaluated certain achievements as Thomas Jesse Jones, supported by Anson Phelps Stokes,

has desired to have them recorded. For this reason
Thomas Jesse Jones, supported by Anson Phelps Stokes,
secretly circulated in 1923 a most scurrilous attack on
the work of the Association among all persons who were
known to contribute to its support.

The immediate result was that one agency thus
appealed to ceased thereafter to give the Association the
annual allowance of $5,000 which it had prior to that
time appropriated. Another thus stirred up withheld
therefrom a contribution of $200.00, and a gentleman
similarly moved withdrew his contribution of $100.00 a
year. We have further evidence of various other ways in
which the work of the Association has thus been
impeded, but such details cannot be set forth in a letter.

If the Phelps Stokes Fund were really interested in the
Negro this foundation would most assuredly spend its
money not in opposition to the work of the only learned
society which the Negroes of this country have organized
and promoted and the one agency which has collected
and published more facts of Negro history than any other
in the world. After the chairmaniof [sic] the Phelps Stokes
Fund had called together his selected group of leaders and
scholars there prevailed a motion from the floor that I be
invited to the conference. Neither he nor his immediate
co-workers, however, desired my cooperation, for they did
not put my name on the original list. The very fact that
they ignored the Association for the Study of Negro Life
and History, the outstanding actor in doing the very thing
which they proposed to do, shows very clearly what their
motives are.

The whole situation is very clear to me, and I sincerely
hope that you will give it enough consideration to
understand it. It is undoubtedly an effort to supplant the
work of the Association in the mind of the public with a
new evaluation of the Negro by these self-appointed
leaders who hope to shape the destiny of the Negro race
in the modern world. If they can secure the cooperation

of the outstanding Negroes who have been invited to participate in this performance they may do much in reaching this end just as Thomas Jesse Jones did in the production of his report on Negro Education which set back the wheels of progress in that particular sphere for almost a generation.

I am, therefore, urging all thinking Negroes and white persons cooperating with them not to take this fatal step. The effect of it will be seen in years to come but then it will be too late. The time has come for the Negro to look out for himself, to construct his own program and carry it out as he sees and understands it. Proposals like these coming from without from those who have already done the race much harm should be looked upon as gifts brought by the Greeks.

I am in no sense opposed to interracial cooperation. I am very much in favor of it. We have it here in promoting the work of the Association for the Study of Negro Life and History. White men contribute to our support and scholars of every race make literary contributions to the JOURNAL OF NEGRO HISTORY from year to year. The program of the Association for the Study of Negro Life and History, however, is conceived by Negroes; and liberal minded members of the other race assist us in the only natural way of helping us to help ourselves.

What do you suppose the Italians of this country would say to the Jews if they proposed to write an Encyclopedia of this element and came to them to have their scholars and leaders endorse the plan to carry out such a project? They would tell them the same thing that the Negroes should say today to the Phelps Stokes Fund or to any other such organization with such a proposal, namely that we should be glad to have any person sufficiently interested in our people to provide funds for a scientific appraisal of their achievements but by no means would we tolerate their evaluation by persons from without who do not appreciate the feeling, thought, and aspirations of the Negro and, therefore, cannot think black.

> Respectfully yours,
> C. G. Woodson,
> Director.

AND THE NEGRO LOSES HIS SOUL

Carter G. Woodson, "And the Negro Loses His Soul," *The Chicago Defender*, national edition, June 25, 1932, 14

Woodson describes some of the moral objectives of education. He also recalls essential lessons he learned from his formerly enslaved and illiterate father.

Observations

THE TREND OF CURRENT THOUGHT AND DISCUSSION

Reading the newspapers, I see that Miss Marian Cuthbert has succeeded Miss Eva D. Bowles in her former position of promoting segregation in the name of God. I have never seen Miss Cuthbert, but, judging from her pictures, I would say that she is a pretty good looking girl, and the boys will enjoy casting wistful eyes at her as she goes on her way working out our undoing for the mess of pottage offered.

Miss Cuthbert will receive a high salary and her assistants will likewise be amply compensated for the unchristian work which they will perform in the further debasement of the Negroes through segregation. If Miss Cuthbert is the sort of woman they say she is, however, she will not give her life to an undesirable effort of this sort. Our Negro women cannot get out of the ghetto under direction of the Y. W. C. A. which consigns them to the ghetto. We need self-controlled hospices for our women under the direction of Negroes, and liberal whites will help us to build them.

Miss Cuthbert should join me in the work of the Association for the Study of Negro Life and History and try to stimulate the Negro women to independent thought and action. We need in this work some good woman with the efficiency and vision of Daisy E. Lampkin to organize the women of the country to think and do for themselves rather than go through the back door of a Jim Crowing establishment to eat the crumbs from its table.

Laboring at this task, however, such a woman worker with us would receive only meager compensation. She might not be sure of more than $12.50 a week and expenses, and sometimes she might have to go hungry. But a life of usefulness under such circumstances is so much more honorable than compromising on principle to obtain the gewgaws and toys of life, for "what shall it profit a man, if he shall gain the whole world, and lose his own soul?"

I am just beginning to understand what this means. When I was a boy seeking religion in Virginia, my white and Colored spiritual advisers left me under the impression that the soul is a piece of flesh, and if you do not have it saved it will be fried to a crisp or burnt to ashes in the lake of fire and brimstone. From my father, however, I learned better than that. He had been a field slave and could neither read nor write, but he proved to be the greatest factor in my education. He joined the church, but never made much noise about it. He never seemed worried about his soul's going to hell. He was more concerned about keeping out of hell on earth.

This former slave, an illiterate man, taught me that you do not have to wait until you die to think about losing your soul. He insisted that when you learn to accept insult, to compromise on principle, to mislead your fellow man, or to betray your people, you have lost your soul. You are already damned.

He taught his children to be polite to everybody but to insist always on recognition as human beings; and, if necessary, fight to the limit for it. Do not do for the traducer of the race anything he will do for you. Do not curry his horse, and grin at him for a favor. Do not brush his hat with one hand while holding out the other for a tip. Do not clean his spittoons for the pittance which he offers. Do not serve in his kitchen for the refuse from his table. Do not shine his shoes to get the worn-out ones for yourself. Do not serve him as a scullion for his cast-off clothing. He often said to me, "I had to do these things when I was a slave. If I continue to do them, I am not a free man. If you do these things you cannot look the oppressor in the eye and say, 'Sir, I am your equal.' Neither he nor you will believe it."

Dangerous doctrine this was, you will say. How can the Negro make a living without rendering such menial service? Well, this former slave raised nine children and did it. Certainly the college men, most of whom have few children, ought to be able to do as well as a former slave. Of course, this required an idealism based upon the greatest sacrifice. Often I remember that I had only one garment and had to go to bed early on Saturday night that my mother might wash this and iron it over night. In this way only I would have something clean to wear to Sunday school. Often during the winter and early in spring we did not have sufficient food, and we would leave the table hungry to go to the woods to pluck the persimmons which the birds had pierced with their beaks and left on the trees. Sometimes in the fields we had to eat the sour grass that grew early in spring out of the providence of God.

In spite of this poverty, however, my father believed that such a life was more honorable than to serve some one as a menial. While his children remained under his vine and fig tree, then, he never hired one to anybody; he never permitted one to wear anybody's cast-off clothing; and he never permitted one to go to any man's back door. If the business could not be transacted through the front door, we had no business with that person. This illiterate freedman realized that the white man had reached his position of influence and power by taking the stand he maintained on these principles, and that the Negro will never amount to anything until he learns to do the same. This was my religious education, and in this way my soul was saved.

I went to school later and learned from books, that Negroes have never been anything and never will be, and, therefore, should accept the status of recognized inferiority. I have seen Negroes thus miseducated champion the cause of segregation in church and state. This sort of training, however, has never registered on me. The education given me by my father, the former slave, has determined my course of life.

It is not a rosy path at all, and sometimes I have to struggle to keep going, but I like it much better than I do the work of a friend of mine who has just accepted a job of segregation paying him $500 a month. He has a new home now. He has recently bought a fine car; and his wife, formerly rejected by the elite, is now breaking through the barriers of "society." His children, too, are going to the best schools in the country, but I wonder what they are preparing themselves for. By the time they reach maturity the effects of just what their father is doing for the profits of segregation may mean the restriction of Negroes altogether to bootlegging, racketeering and prostitution.

The progress of this evil has been one fatal step after another. We accepted segregation in the schools to get jobs. Then we accepted it in the civil service because we had to make a living. Next we had segregation in the cities. Following this came segregation in rural areas. This has finally led to the proposal to have the races on different continents; but, since the white man has taken over Africa, some one will have to discover a new continent for the Negro or exterminate him altogether. This sad plight has resulted from our compromising leadership. If the Negroes could chloroform about 99 percent of their superimposed leaders the Race might survive. Under them we are gaining one thing while losing the only thing that makes life worthwhile. "What shall it profit a man, if he shall gain the whole world, and lose his own soul?"

DIFFERENTIATION IN EDUCATION
WITH RESPECT TO RACES

Carter G. Woodson, "Differentiation in Education
with Respect to Races," *The New York Age*,
January 27, 1934, 5

Woodson insists that the study of racial inequality should
be taken on in explicit terms in schools, especially for black
students.

I learn that the "great leaders of thought" are working out a
"differentiation" in education with respect to races. I do not
believe in any such policy. We should teach the Negro the
same way that we teach any other race and essentially the
same things that we would teach any other race.

(This is the first of a series of articles on this subject).

We teach the white child about himself and about others in
relation to himself. This method is right. However, we teach
the Negro child about the white race and about others in relation to the white race. Such approach is wrong. The procedure
in the one case should be the same as that in the other. Every
element of our population should be taught to develop from
within rather than have so much disorganized and unrelated
matter poured in from without. The failure to do this in the
training of the Negro has made his education largely a failure.

I see a danger in "differentiation in education with respect to
races," for it carries the idea of a superimposed program with
possibilities of invidious distinctions. This was the original policy in dealing with the Negro in other matters. Some years ago,
however, the Negroes had a free-for-all fight among themselves
about the kind of education they should have, although they
did not actually acquire much of any sort. The whites had
never been very much concerned about it; but, on becoming interested, they accepted one of the views of the two Negro factions and tried to carry it out. Now the whites are doing their
own thinking about Negro education. They are setting up
Negro educators here and there to do what they want to see

carried out. We very readily serve them, for it supplies temporary relief to the Negro agent thus fattened, although this policy may so far remove the other members of the race from the
public trough as to force them into the bread line.

This recent thought about the Negro results from his present
plight. In this country he has always been a parasite hanging
on to the white man upon whom he has lived by doing his
drudgery. Now that drudgery has been eliminated by machinery, the white man brushes aside his Negro parasite who must
go to the bread line where he is gradually starving. How then
should we educate people who are thus doomed? It is useless to
teach the Negro the mechanic arts because trades unions have
proscribed him in such spheres. It is unwise to train them in
business administration because the Communists are rapidly
destroying capital. It is not necessary to teach the Negro Hebrew unless there is some advantage in knowing how to beg for
bread in that language. It is hardly profitable to teach the Negro
the culture of the ancients unless in their philosophy he may
find some consolation while suffering from the pangs of hun-
ger. It will be useless even to teach the Negro local geography
unless it is considered advantageous for him to know that running the bread line in one town will be more profitable than
standing in line in another. If Negroes do not need any education at all, teachers of their schools will be unnecessary, as recently argued a man in support of a motion to disestablish a
Negro State College; and it failed by only one vote. If Negroes
continue to turn atheistic and leave the church because it has
substituted the ideals of Hertzog and Hitler for those of Jesus
of Nazareth, there will be no need for Negro preachers. In the
other higher spheres the members are considered so small that
Negroes thus occupied may be easily dispensed with.

Since the Negro has actually become worthless to the white
lords in the machine age some have inquired as to why they
should not hasten process of extermination by sterilization as
devised by Hitler for his undesirables. The propagation of this
particular species would thus be brought to an end by an apparently humane method which is so much more effective than
birth-control, and what is now being present to educate and

elevate Negroes could be profitably used to keep alive those left to read their doom in the setting sun. Our race, then, should be congratulated, at least, for making others think, although, the process does not have that effect on us. If we ever learn to think we shall have our own program of education.

In the first place, I would teach the Negro child. I say child because there is little or no hope for the Negroes who are beyond thirty. They have been so developed as to continue content with the incidents of slavery and the badges of inferiority. Negroes of this finish cannot be expected to do any more than to underestimate and destroy the teachers of their schools, the pastors of their churches, the professional men around them, and the business men in their communities. The goal of their lives will be to connect themselves with others in exclusive circles; and, if they finally penetrate such spheres only to find that they are not desirable, they will sour on life and become stumbling blocks to progress.

I would begin with the Negro child himself and then take up his environment as an index to his activities. This is the natural order for all education. If conditions around the Negro child are undesirable or even intolerable I would not try to hide these things from him. I would inform him accordingly just as soon as he developed the power to see and observe things for himself. I would try to show wherein these conditions have resulted from unsound policies and unwise methods; I would endeavor to stimulate in him the ambition to do something concrete to correct the evils which surround him. I would teach him history, the great stimulus in the present and monitor to the future. Out of it this child must learn that present day conditions now afflicting the Negro are not worse than similar difficulties which have handicapped other peoples who since that day have extricated themselves therefrom and have made a deep impression upon their time.

I would teach this Negro child that he is black, but comely, black and beautiful, and even beautifully black! While others on the street, through the press, and on the rostrum are trying to make him accept his color as a mark of inferiority I would show by the achievement of his forebears that they measured up in their glorious record to the level of the greatest peoples of the world. I would deliberately teach the Negro child the falsity of the doctrines which have prevented the clear thinking of people of today. I would sound the keynote of hope in the African proverb, "Lies however numerous will be caught by truth when it rises up." I would say to the Negro child as does the African, "Know thyself better than he who speaks of thee. Not to know is bad, not to wish to know is worse." For the literature of the Teutons I would find a parallel in the rich treasures in the lore of the African. I would place the African words of wisdom in the class with those of the Greek philosophers. I would classify Es-Sadi with Homer, Antar with Shakespeare, Askia with Julius Caesar, and Askia the Great with Augustus. In short, I would inspire the Negro rather than crush in him the bud of genius by a so-called "education."

MY RECOLLECTIONS OF VETERANS
OF THE CIVIL WAR

Carter G. Woodson, "My Recollections of Veterans of the Civil War," *Negro History Bulletin*, February 1944, 103–15

This essay is one of Woodson's most extensive treatments of his early life and education. He reflects on being taught by his formerly enslaved uncles and describes his time laboring alongside Civil War veterans whose personal stories cultivated his interest in studying black life and history.

The veteran of the Civil War best known to me was my father, James Henry Woodson. He was owned as a slave in Fluvanna County on the James River about sixty-five miles above Richmond, Virginia, in one of the infertile sections of worn-out hilly land and on that side of the stream which in its meandering aggravated the situation by leaving the alluvial soil on the opposite side of the river. In this infelicitous situation planters often had more slaves than could make a living on their own premises and hired out their surplus bondmen. Because of this misfortune, James Henry Woodson, although of a mechanical turn, like his father, Carter Woodson who was a cabinet maker, was debased to the level of a ditch-digger in the employ of one James Stratton. The son, making use of his mechanical knowledge, picked up mainly by contact and observation, was at this time hewing from the forest nearby some hard timber out of which he made at night rough furniture and fish traps which he sold for pocket change. Learning that the bondman was thus applying his leisure, Stratton came upon him in the ditch where he was working one morning and undertook to whip the employee for thus exploiting his opportunity. The employee, however, turned the scales, whipped Stratton, and rushed back to the plantation where he was owned by one Jack Toney.

Seeing James returning home, Toney indignantly inquired:

"What are you doing here this time of day?"

"Stratton and I fell out," was the reply.

"Fell out! That's the trouble now! All free! All free!"

"Yes, we are free," came the retort. "And if you bother me I'll kill you, another devil!"

The rebellious slave, realizing his danger, rushed to his cabin, grabbed his best suit of clothes and a clean white handkerchief, dashed toward the woods where he quickly dressed in this more becoming attire and made his way as rapidly as possible toward Richmond. He had heard that the Union Soldiers, or the Yankees, as they were called, were in that area. He hurried on and on, hoping to see some trace of the friends of freedom. Finally he began to hear the tramping of horses and on entering a wide field he saw in the distance a cavalry detachment dressed in blue. When the Captain Marks in charge saw the fugitive he yelled out, "Halt." The fugitive had learned that, if he waved something white that would mean no offense, and he would not be mistaken for an enemy. Thereupon he waved his white handkerchief to great effect, and the officer beckoned him to come hither. With a heart leaping for joy the fugitive rushed to the invading troops.

"Who are you?" inquired the officer. "A runaway slave?"

"Yes, Sir. I had to escape for my life because to prevent my employer from beating me I had to beat him."

"Mount that horse. Fall in line and come with us. Where is this man that treated you so cruelly?"

"His name is Stratton, and he lives only a few miles up the river. I'll show you."

And they rode on to the Stratton plantation, caught the owner, tied him up and whipped him. They even made him climb a tree backwards. Then, using the fugitive as a guide, the invaders directed their raid farther into the interior of the state.

"Do you know of any stores of provisions and other materials of war?" inquired the captain.

"I do," said the fugitive, giving in detail what he knew about the supplies at the mills near Fork Union in Fluvanna County.

The troops were soon on the very spot but found the place guarded by Confederate soldiers. The invaders called on the defenders to surrender, but they indignantly refused. The order was promptly given to fire, and after the exchange of a few shots resulting in the death of a disproportionate number of the defenders the remainder took flight to the neighboring woods. The invaders loaded on their horses all the provisions they could conveniently carry and burned all the rest. This act they repeated here and there on that raid and then returned to the Richmond-Petersburg area where under Philip H. Sheridan, after his dashes east and west they participated in the final maneuvers which forced the surrender of Robert E. Lee. James Henry Woodson served the rest of the war under Captain Marks and the famous Custer who years later made his last charge among the Indians in the Far West. After emancipation, however, the freedman settled in Buckingham County, Virginia, where he married Anne Eliza Riddle in 1867.

Another member of my family enlightened me considerably on the Civil War. He was my mother's brother, Robert D. Riddle, who was born in Buckingham County across the James River from Fluvanna County. As a small child he was sold with his mother to the planter near Buchanan in what is now the western part of Virginia. The poor and indebted slaveholders had tried to show compassion in trying not to sell the mother from her little children; and my mother, Anne Eliza Riddle, then a girl of only eleven years, persuaded the owners to sell her instead and thus keep the little children and their mother together. However, although they placed Anne Eliza twice on the slave block at Buckingham Court House and once in Richmond they could not secure for her such a price as would relieve the plantation of the pressing debt. As a last resort they placed the mother of the children on the block and sold her and the two youngest of her offspring for $2,300 which brought relief to the impoverished owners. Robert D. Riddle was the older of these two children.

Not many years thereafter came the Civil War, and Union Soldiers in one of their raids into the interior of Virginia, very much like the one mentioned above, reached the plantation where they saw this interesting little mulatto running around the cabin while his mother was toiling in the fields. He so impressed these men that they took him along as a mascot. His people, however, never learned what became of him and mourned him as one destroyed by some natural force, probably devoured by the wild beasts.

On reaching mountainous West Virginia these soldiers found that they could not properly care for such a young boy and gave him to a colored family at White Sulphur Springs. They could never find out exactly what his origin was because the boy was so young when taken from his parents that he remembered only his mother's name and his own—Robert D. Riddle. In 1873, however, a solution came when his oldest sister, Anne Eliza Woodson, at that time the wife of James Henry Woodson, had moved with her husband to West Virginia, where he was engaged in the construction of the Chesapeake and Ohio Railroad through West Virginia and later figured as a laborer in the development of Huntington. To that new settlement came persons from afar and among them a worker who had been brought up at White Sulphur Springs. Having heard Mrs. Woodson speak frequently of her lost brother, this worker recalled that a young man at his former home had that very name and resembled Mrs. Woodson. He addressed to his home town a detailed inquiry and thereby discovered this lost brother.

Great rejoicing followed in Huntington when this young man came to visit his sister and likewise in Buckingham County, Virginia, to which his mother had returned immediately after the Civil War with the younger child, John Morton Riddle. Robert D. Riddle remained in West Virginia where he was educated and later taught school at Ronceverte. He finally distinguished himself by maintaining a family of five in cultivating exceptionally fine celery on a small parcel of only one acre.

One of the most interesting veterans of the Civil War with whom I came into contact and one of the best friends I have ever had I fortunately met at Nutallburg, Fayette County, West Virginia, where I became a coal miner. (I was not born in West Virginia. My parents moved in 1874 from Huntington, West Virginia, back to their old home near New Canton in Buckingham County Virginia. There I was born the following year. At that time, however, Virginia, like most of the worn-out South, was passing through an age of poverty, and to escape the hardships which endured in that state younger Negroes went as workers to build railroads and open the coal mines of West Virginia, Kentucky, and Ohio. My oldest brother, Robert H. Woodson, had gone in this migration, and on returning home on a visit in Virginia he gave such a glowing account of the prosperity to the west that all the children wanted to go with him to this land of promise. My mother was easily induced to go, but it was only with reluctance that my father agreed to go back to the Little Mountain State. After my brother and I spent a short time helping to build the railroad from Thurmond up Loup Creek in 1892 we found more desirable employment as coal miners at Nutallburg in Fayette County and moved the family back to Huntington in 1893.)

This veteran was Oliver Jones. He had had experience as a cook in his native Richmond before the Civil War, and in his new home in West Virginia he made himself useful as a restaurateur. After doing a day's work in the coal mine he would throw his home open as a tearoom for the miners. This was a godsend for these men. The operators who owned all the land around would never allow the establishment of any business to compete with their commissary where they sold the essentials of life at prices from sixty to one hundred percent higher than they were offered elsewhere. There was, however, no objection to Oliver Jones' selling ice cream, fruits, and especially water-melons which he bought by the car loads. Inasmuch as I always enjoyed nice things to eat I frequented this place, and there I made a great friend.

Jones was the very sort of man to have charge of a resort of this type. In the first place, he was a fine-looking man—a mulatto of dark-brown hair and chestnut eyes, with a well trained mustache and becoming goatee. He stood about five feet eight inches tall and was slightly bowlegged, a condition aggravated somewhat by an all but fatal accident in the mine. He looked the part of a Virginia gentleman. He never had much to say except in the case of matters of importance on which he could speak intelligently. He was a well educated man, but he could neither read nor write. He learned through others who had had opportunities for intellectual development. When I met him I had just come out of Virginia where I had had the good fortune of being well grounded in the fundamentals taught in the rural schools of my native home by my two uncles, John Morton Riddle and James Buchanan Riddle. When Oliver Jones learned that I could read he soon engaged me to inform him and his friends as to what was in the daily newspapers. My compensation was to have all the nice things I wanted to eat. Whenever a veteran of the Civil War came out as a candidate for office or achieved distinction, I had to look him up in the books, inform my friends as to what battles he had fought, victories he had won and principles which he thereafter sustained. Jones was especially anxious to hear about those veterans who, like himself, were in battle array to attack Lee's army the morning he surrendered at Appomattox Court House.

This service for a friend was decidedly educational for me. I learned so much myself because of the much more extensive reading required by him than I probably would have undertaken for my own benefit. This reading was not a new task for me, for in Virginia, as the youngest boy of the family, the last to be permitted to go into life to make an independent living, I had thus served my father. Yet, in Virginia newspapers did not circulate freely. Negroes and poor whites could not spare funds for such a purpose, and we had to depend upon stale news. In West Virginia, however, the situation was very different. Miners usually made more money than they knew what to do with, and thousands wasted their earnings in whiskey, gambling and playing the role of desperados. Oliver Jones and his circle represented the better type. He would take a social glass among friends, but never indulged himself to excess. He would never offer me anything to drink. To him it was a bad habit. Do not begin it, and you will not have to end it.

Oliver Jones' home was all but a reading room. He bought interesting books on the Negro—J. T. Wilson's *Black Phalanx*, W. J. Simmons' *Men of Mark*, G. W. Williams' *Negro Troops in the War of the Rebellion* and others giving the important achievements of the Negro. He subscribed to the Negro newspapers like *The Mountainer* and *The Pioneer*, edited in the State by Christopher Payne; and *The Richmond Planet*, edited by John Mitchell at Richmond. When these and other distinguished Negroes came to town they visited Oliver Jones, and there I had the opportunity to learn something about the trials and battles of the Negro for freedom and equality. Jones had fought for those principles as a soldier in the Civil War, and he was still willing to do his part to further the cause. In this circle the history of the race was discussed frequently, and my interest in penetrating the past of my people was deepened and intensified.

This circle, however, was not narrowly confined to the discussion of the trials and afflictions of the race. Oliver Jones was a liberal-minded man seeking to broaden his vision by keeping up with whatever passed in this country and in remote parts of the universe. He subscribed to such papers as the Pittsburgh *Telegraph*, the Toledo *Blade*, the Cincinnati *Commercial Gazette*, the *Enquirer* and the Louisville *Courier Journal*. We knew about such outstanding editors as Murat Halstead, John R. McClean and Henry Watterson. Occasionally we got inklings of Samuel Bowles of the Springfield *Republican*, of Charles A. Dana of the New York *Sun*, and of Whitelaw Reid of the New York *Tribune*. We learned much thereby about the issues before the American people and the measures offered to meet the demands of the times. In these newspapers which I read to Oliver Jones were speeches, lectures and essays dealing with civil service reform, reduction of taxes, tariff for protection, tariff for revenue only and free trade. We had the opportunity to learn through the press about the gold standard, bimetallism, the demonetization of silver, and the free and unlimited coinage of silver at the legal ratio of 16 to 1. Along with these came the new leaders of Populist doctrines with such thoughts as those of "Sockless" Jere Simpson of Kansas, Tom Watson of Georgia, and William Jennings Bryan of Nebraska in the wave of primary elections, the recall of judges, initiative and referendum, and the curbing of monopolies by government ownership. In seeking through the press information on these questions for Oliver Jones and his friends I was learning in an effective way most important phases of history and economies.

I had the opportunity to continue this education under another Civil War veteran in Huntington to which I went in 1895 to attend the Douglass High School and of which I became principal in 1900. My father still required me to read for him just as I had done first for him in Virginia and for Oliver Jones later in West Virginia. From this valuable experience my practical education continued.

Another veteran was a Confederate named Wysong. My father worked under him as a foreman at the Chesapeake and Ohio Railway Shops in Huntington. On many occasions he and my father discussed the Civil War and other veterans joined the conversation. The discussion was especially profitable on Sunday morning when there was not much to do. Although I was a man of twenty-five and the principal of the local high school, my mother would order me to take my father a warm breakfast on Sunday morning that he might feast just as we did on the steaks, chops and fowl we usually had on Sunday morning. I was glad of the opportunity, for I soon found myself learning so much about the Civil War from the actual participants that I sought rather than neglected the opportunity to carry the dinner pail. These discussions were suddenly brought to a close when in one of the debates Wysong, the Confederate, played up unduly the Lost Cause or defended slavery too boldly. My father engaged him in a fisticuff in which the employee got the better of the boss. Wysong vehemently demanded the dismissal of the victor. The master mechanic in charge did not take any such action, but gave instruction to the effect that there should be no more discussion of the issues of the Civil War.

In Huntington I met another great veteran of the Civil War. This was George T. Prosser, who at the turn of the century was building a successful African Methodist Episcopal Church in Huntington, West Virginia. Up to that day the Negroes in this city had had only a large Baptist Church and an average size Methodist Church, controlled by the white organization of the North. Prosser came and told the people about the independent religious movement among Negroes and the dignity given their church by their own intelligent leaders. The people heeded his message; and, although he had a difficult task, he secured a following which assured the future of his work in that city.

Prosser was the man for this task. He was a native of Harrisburg, Pennsylvania, where he early had the advantage of education. He was no philosopher or theologian, but he spoke good English and could exhort well from the Bible and his unusual experience. He was decidedly fortunate in being a man of striking personality. He stood about six feet in a well proportioned body—a black man with features varying between those of the African and the Arab. He had a beautiful voice, and in both preaching and singing he was a commanding figure.

As a young man Prosser volunteered from his native city because he had been sorely disappointed in love by a woman who expressed her preference for another fellow of his circle. To drown his sorrow he joined the Massachusetts Fifty-Fourth Regiment which was taking shape under the command of Colonel Robert Gould Shaw. After brief training these soldiers were sent to the front to make the charge at Fort Wagner where most of them were taken as prisoners or like their gallant leader, were mowed down under accurate fire of the Confederate cannon July 19, 1863. Prosser was made a prisoner and was thus held until the close of the war. His account of the hardships which he experienced is all but torture itself. The Negro prisoners were poorly clad, poorly fed, and sometimes all but starved. The white prisoners, who were better cared for, would occasionally give the Negro prisoners a part of their pittance in return for "cutting a shine" or some sort of antics to excite their sympathy. At times, he said, they had such little meat that they had to gnaw the leather of old shoes and were even reduced to the extremity of eating dog meat.

One of the most impressive sermons I have ever listened to was one delivered by Prosser on his experiences in the Civil War. His climax was that when he was finally delivered from prison the Federal Government gave him back pay for every day he spent in prison, for the food that he was not allowed to eat, for the shoes that he was not permitted to wear, and for the clothes that he was denied. God, he said, would thus reward the faithful Christian who served Him in this life.

In the years that followed I met hundreds of Civil War Veterans, but fortunately, or unfortunately, I had attended college where I was directed toward definitive history—away from the personal narrative and the romantic aspects of the conflict. In Washington, D.C., where I have spent most of my time during the last thirty-five years I had the opportunity to know Lewis Douglass and Charles R. Douglass, sons of Frederick Douglass, who served in the Civil War. I knew of Major Fleetwood who had the same experience and Dr. Charles B. Purvis who attained the rank of surgeon in the Union Army. With one exception it was not my opportunity to secure from more recent acquaintances stories which had an unusual human interest, although I am sure that their accounts would have been just as interesting as these herein related.

The exception to which I refer is Pinckney Benton Stewart Pinchback whom I knew well and with whom I often talked about the past. When I first met the "Governor" as we were accustomed to call him, I did not know how to take him. I had heard much about him through his enemies and had some misgivings in approaching him. By becoming acquainted with the man I learned that he had been misrepresented by his antagonists whom he had outwitted in the game of politics in Louisiana during the Reconstruction. In spite of their methods of shady and questionable order Pinchback secured election to the Constitutional convention, contrived to be chosen for both branches of the State legislature, to be Lieutenant Governor, to serve as the Acting Governor of the State, and to be elected to the United States Senate from which the politicians of both parties barred him, although his title thereafter was conceded as valid and he drew full pay. This rapid rise made him anathema to the agents of racial minority rule who branded him as a corrupt leader. Investigation, however, shows that he was an honest man who deserved the plaudits of his countrymen.

With respect to the Civil War Pinchback's account was very enlightening. He used to relate with much feeling his experiences in Ohio where he contrived to attend Gilmore's High School but soon came to want when the heirs to his white father's estate deprived him and his mother of their share. His struggle to make a living and to assist his mother with an invalid son took him steamboating which during those antebellum days before the rise of railroads was considerably profitable. The turning point in his career was in 1861 when his work as a steward on the steamboat was interrupted by the Civil War. Pinchback felt that in the midst of the fight in his native New Orleans he could do something to help the advance of freedom. In Yazoo, Mississippi, on May 10, 1862, therefore, Pinchback abandoned the steamer on which he was serving, ran the Confederate blockade, and reached the Crescent City. There he soon became involved in trouble with his brother-in-law who had Pinchback imprisoned for assault. From this, however, he soon emerged. He was released to enlist in the First Louisiana Volunteer Infantry. Soon thereafter he was commissioned to assist in recruiting the Louisiana Second Infantry. Next came the call of General Benjamin Butler, the commander of the department of the Gulf, urging colored men to enlist and fight to save the Union.

Thereafter Pinchback was to continue the recruiting under more favorable circumstances, but there arose difficulties of mustering these Negro troops into the service. The Second Regiment Native Guards with Pinchback commanding Company A was recognized October 12, 1862. Yet difficulty lay in the fact that the Union soldiers were about as much prejudiced against the Negro soldiers as were the Confederates. Pinchback

insisted on equal treatment and equal compensation for soldiers regardless of their color, but he became so discouraged in
the rising tide of race hate that he and his fellow officers resigned before the end of the first year. Later, after another conference with General N. P. Banks, Pinchback took new courage
and organized a company of Negro cavalry; but, although
General Banks was glad to receive the Company, he would not
accept Pinchback as the officer of the unit. His excuse was that
no authority then existed for the employment of Negroes in
any other capacity than that of privates. Rebuffed but not yet
despairing, Pinchback, accompanied by Captain H. C. Carter,
came to Washington in 1865 to obtain permission from President Lincoln to raise a regiment of colored men in Ohio and
Indiana, but the end of the war came before this plan could be
considered by the administration.

THOMAS JESSE JONES

Carter G. Woodson, "Thomas Jesse Jones,"
The Journal of Negro History 35, no. 1
(January 1950): 107–9

In this obituary, Woodson described the long career of
Thomas Jesse Jones, an ideological leader among white philanthropists who strongly influenced their strategies for
funding black education. According to Woodson, Jones's
ideas led most African Americans "to consider him an evil
in the life of the Negro."

On the fifth of January Thomas Jesse Jones, a career man in
Negro Life, died. He was born in Wales on August 4, 1873
and claimed relationship with Lloyd George, the premier of
England during the First World War. Jones came to the United
States in 1884. He attended Washington and Lee University in
Virginia one year. He next attended Marietta College in
Ohio where he received the Bachelor of Arts degree in 1897.
He did graduate work leading to the degree of Doctor of

Philosophy at Columbia and studied theology at Union Theological Seminary.

Jones began his career as a social settlement worker in New York City. He next did research work at Hampton Institute in Virginia. He was chosen later to participate in the compilation of statistics bearing especially upon the Negro in connection with the census taken in 1910. Next he became the director of the educational survey of Negro schools sponsored by the Phelps Stokes Fund in cooperation with the United States Department of Education. The results of this survey were published in two volumes in 1917. A conference was called to meet in Washington, D.C. for a thorough discussion of this report. Those attending showed a wide difference of opinion as to its value. Taking the well established and amply supported Hampton Institute as his criterion, Jones reported as questionable and unworthy of support many of the struggling Negro schools which, although below standard, had educated and inspired thousands of Negroes who would not have received any education at all if these schools had not been established and maintained on a lower level.

This fault in Jones' judgment led most Negroes to consider him an evil in the life of the Negro; but he was nevertheless, catapulted into fame among the capitalists and government officials supporting the education of Negroes. They made Jones the almoner of the despised race with the title of Educational Director of the Phelps Stokes Fund which he served from 1913 to 1946. When he said do not give here and do not help yonder the "philanthropic" element heeded his biddings. He became immediately successful as the most advanced agent of Negro control. It developed as a dreadful machine using the Phelps Stokes Fund to finance espionage. He appeared at Negro assemblies and had his co-workers to function likewise in keeping abreast of the thought of the Negro to find out whom to help and whom to destroy. By granting Negro administrators from a hundred to two hundred each annually he assured himself sufficient support among them to make it appear that he was acceptable to most of the race. His published works on his efforts and results therefrom were of the type claiming credit for what others had achieved.

Later Jones transferred his operations to Africa. He easily ingratiated himself into the favor of the few European agencies working for the enlightenment of the Natives within the locus prescribed by economic imperialists. Agencies in the United States, thinking well of Jones as a most Christian gentleman thus giving his life as a sacrifice for the uplift of the poor, willingly supplemented the meager funds of the Phelps Stokes Fund to make his program for Africa feasible. Jones assisted those missions and other agencies in Africa which met his approval, but made in Africa the same blunder which he had made in the United States in trying to block the efforts of other agencies which did not please him. For two years a word from Jones kept Max Yergan out of South Africa after his sponsors and co-workers had made available the funds to finance his mission there. Jones conducted a campaign against the Association for the Study of Negro Life and History because its Director questioned the wisdom of Jones' African policy. By 1930 he succeeded in lopping off all support of the Association from boards and foundations. Jones, however, did succeed in establishing in Africa the Achimota College, modeled after Hampton and developed under a white educator with J. E. J. Aggrey, an educated African, as his assistant. The untimely death of Aggrey somewhat frustrated these plans, but the school has endured to achieve a measure of success.

To say that Jones did not accomplish some good in the various positions which he filled would be far from the truth. He would have achieved greater success, however, if he had not been so narrow-minded, short-sighted, vindictive and undermining. His clandestine methods of hamstringing defeated his own purposes. He operated altogether behind closed doors. Rarely would a Negro leader in the United States speak commendably of such an unscrupulous man. So many Africans turned against him that he failed to establish a control over all the African students coming to the United States for education, and certain missionary agencies refused to follow his biddings. His career is a fair warning to others of the white race to employ different methods in dealing with the self-asserting Negro.

Suggestions for Further Reading

Anderson, James. *The Education of Blacks in the South: 1860–1935.* Chapel Hill: University of North Carolina Press, 1988.

Dagbovie, Pero G. "'Among the Vitalizing Tools of the Radical Intelligentsia, of Course the Most Crucial Was Words': Carter G. Woodson's 'The Case of the Negro' (1921)." *Journal for the Study of Radicalism* 3, no. 2 (2009): 81–112.

Dagbovie, Pero G. "Black Women, Carter G. Woodson, and the Association for the Study of Negro Life and History, 1915–1950." *The Journal of African American History* 88, no. 1 (January 1, 2003): 21.

Dagbovie, Pero G. *Carter G. Woodson in Washington, D.C.: Father of Black History.* Charleston, SC: Arcadia Publishing, 2014.

Dagbovie, Pero G. *The Early Black History Movement, Carter G. Woodson, and Lorenzo Johnston Greene.* Urbana: University of Illinois Press, 2007.

Givens, Jarvis R. *Fugitive Pedagogy: Carter G. Woodson and the Art of Black Teaching.* Cambridge, MA: Harvard University Press, 2021.

Givens, Jarvis R. "'He Was, Undoubtedly, a Wonderful Character': Black Teachers' Representations of Nat Turner During Jim Crow." *Souls* 18, nos. 2–4 (October 1, 2016): 215–34.

Givens, Jarvis R. "'There Would Be No Lynching If It Did Not Start in the Schoolroom': Carter G. Woodson and the Occasion of Negro History Week, 1926–1950." *American Educational Research Journal* 56, no. 4 (2019): 1457–94.

Goggin, Jacqueline. *Carter G. Woodson: A Life in Black History.* Baton Rouge: LSU Press, 1997.

Grant, Carl, Keffrelyn Brown, and Anthony L. Brown. *Black Intellectual Thought in Education: The Missing Traditions of Anna*

Julia Cooper, Carter G. Woodson, and Alain LeRoy Locke. New York: Routledge, 2015.

Greene, Lorenzo J. *Selling Black History for Carter G. Woodson: A Diary, 1930–1933.* Edited by Arvarh E. Strickland. Columbia: University of Missouri, 1996.

Greene, Lorenzo J. *Working with Carter G. Woodson, the Father of Black History: A Diary, 1928–1930.* Edited by Arvarh E. Strickland. Baton Rouge: LSU Press, 1989.

Hine, Darlene Clark. "Carter G. Woodson, White Philanthropy and Negro Historiography." *The History Teacher* 19, no. 3 (1986): 405–25.

King, LaGarrett J., Ryan M. Crowley, and Anthony L. Brown. "The Forgotten Legacy of Carter G. Woodson: Contributions to Multicultural Social Studies and African American History." *The Social Studies* 101, no. 5 (August 23, 2010): 211–15.

Meier, August, and Elliott Rudwick. *Black History and the Historical Profession, 1915–1980.* Urbana: University of Illinois Press, 1986.

Morris, Burnis R. *Carter G. Woodson: History, the Black Press, and Public Relations.* Jackson: University Press of Mississippi, 2017.

Scally, Mary Anthony. *Carter G. Woodson: A Bio-Bibliography.* Westport, CT: Greenwood, 1985.

Snyder, Jeffrey Aaron. *Making Black History: The Color Line, Culture, and Race in the Age of Jim Crow.* Athens: University of Georgia Press, 2018.

Wilson, Francille Rusan. *The Segregated Scholars: Black Social Scientists and the Creation of Black Labor Studies, 1890–1950.* Charlottesville: University of Virginia Press, 2006.

Woodson, Carter Godwin. *African Heroes and Heroines.* Washington, DC: The Associated Publishers, 1939.

Woodson, Carter Godwin. *A Century of Negro Migration.* Washington, DC: The Association for the Study of Negro Life and History, 1918.

Woodson, Carter Godwin. *Negro Makers of History.* Washington, DC: The Associated Publishers, 1928.

Woodson, Carter Godwin. *The Education of the Negro Prior to 1861: A History of the Education of the Colored People of the United States from the Beginning of Slavery to the Civil War.* New York and London: Putnam and Sons, 1915.

Woodson, Carter Godwin. *The Negro in Our History.* Washington, DC: The Associated Publishers, 1922.

Notes

CHAPTER I.
THE SEAT OF THE TROUBLE

1. An ethnic label used to reference people of Germanic descent.

CHAPTER II.
HOW WE MISSED THE MARK

1. Commissioned by Congress in 1865, the Bureau of Refugees, Freedmen, and Abandoned Lands (the Freedmen's Bureau) provisioned schools and social services to the war-torn South. The collaborative effort of the Freedmen's Bureau, private philanthropy, and African American communities established the foundation for tax-funded schooling, an idea widely opposed among Southern leaders.
2. Reconstruction describes the period of U.S. history between the end of the Civil War in 1865 and the Compromise of 1877.
3. In the transition from the nineteenth to the twentieth century, influential corporate philanthropists endorsed an industrial model of education for black students. This satisfied interests to perpetuate the servile relations engendered during slavery in the economy of the industrializing South.
4. Roland Hayes (1887–1977), a tenor, was the first African American man to reach international acclaim as a concert performer; Henry O. Tanner (1859–1937), a painter, achieved recognition within international art circles for the biblical themes rendered in his artwork.

CHAPTER III.
HOW WE DRIFTED AWAY FROM THE TRUTH

1. In the seventeenth century, Abd el-Rahman al-Sa'di composed the *Tarikh al-Sudan*, a detailed history of the Songhay Empire.

CHAPTER IV.
EDUCATION UNDER OUTSIDE CONTROL

1. Atticus Green Haygood (1839–1896), former president of Emory College and agent of the John F. Slater Fund; Jabez Lamar Monroe Curry (1825–1903), agent of the Peabody Fund who would later succeed Haygood as trustee of the Slater Fund; officials such as William Henry Ruffner (1824–1908), superintendent of Public Instruction of Virginia, would rely on private philanthropy to fund and maintain racially segregated schools.
2. Jessie O. Thomas (1885–1972), educator and civil rights leader, was a graduate of Tuskegee and protégé of Booker T. Washington. He later returned to Tuskegee to serve as a field secretary, fundraising in Rochester, New York.
3. Each figure is notable for their contribution to higher education. Dr. Robert Russa Moton (1867–1940) succeeded Booker T. Washington as the second president of Tuskegee Institute from 1915 to 1935; Dr. John Hope (1868–1936) served as the first African American president of both Morehouse College in 1906 and Atlanta University in 1929.
4. John Jasper (1812–1901) was formerly enslaved and gained national prominence for his 1878 sermon "The Sun Do Move." In it he declared the earth was flat and the sun moved. Here, Woodson positions Jasper's folk knowledge as worthy of study, highlighting the importance of engaging black folk knowledge with the same attention and rigor given to Greek mythology.
5. T. M. Campbell (1883–1956) was a joint employee of Tuskegee Institute and the USDA who taught rural farmers advanced methods in farming and land management; B. F. Hubert (1884–1958) served as president of Georgia State Industrial College for Colored Youth, the first publicly run HBCU in the state.

CHAPTER V.
THE FAILURE TO LEARN TO MAKE A LIVING

1. In 1775, the Continental Congress issued the Continental currency to finance the Revolutionary War. Backed by the anticipation of tax revenue, the notes had no backing in gold and silver, giving rise to the phrase "not worth a Continental."

CHAPTER VI.
THE EDUCATED NEGRO LEAVES THE MASSES

1. The concept of "The Talented Tenth" references the idea that a cadre of black intellectuals trained in higher education hold a special role in uplifting the masses of the race. The idea first appears in an essay of that very title published in 1896 by Henry Lyman Morehouse (for whom Morehouse College is named) and was popularized seven years later by W. E. B. Du Bois.
2. Founded in 1909 by Nannie Helen Burroughs, the National Training School for Women and Girls educated black women from around the world. The curriculum reflected Burroughs's dedication to training independent and God-fearing women committed to racial uplift.
3. Old-fashioned or conservative in sensibilities.

CHAPTER VIII.
PROFESSIONAL EDUCATION DISCOURAGED

1. Ira Aldridge (1807–1867), actor, became internationally recognized for his ability to play both the greatest tragic characters of Shakespeare and melodramatic enslaved characters.

CHAPTER IX.
POLITICAL EDUCATION NEGLECTED

1. Oscar DePriest (1871–1951), politician and civil rights activist, served in the U.S. Congress from 1929 to 1935. As part of Negro History Week celebrations in 1932, Woodson brought nearly a thousand children to the House Office to meet Representative DePriest.
2. William Lloyd Garrison (1805–1879) and John Brown (1800–1859) were both prominent white abolitionists in the Anti-Slavery Movement.

3. Elizabeth Donnan (1883–1955), professor of political economy, published *Documents Illustrative of the History of the Slave Trade to America* in four volumes; Helen Tunnicliff Caterall (1870–1933), attorney and historian, published *Judicial Cases Concerning American Slavery and the Negro*; Frederic Bancroft (1860–1945), historian, published *Slave Trading in the Old South*.

4. In 1921, news editor and politician Claude Bowers (1878–1958) published *The Tragic Era*, an account of Reconstruction sympathetic to the cause of the former confederacy. Scholars of the "new Southern school of thought" put forth more favorable accounts of Reconstruction, elevating African Americans' presence and contributions to preserving democracy.

CHAPTER X.
THE LOSS OF VISION

1. In 1816, a group of elite white men funded the American Colonization Society, an organization designed to expel free African Americans from the nation.

2. Charles Lenox Remond (1810–1873), African American abolitionist and civil rights orator, was a prominent member of the Anti-Slavery Society.

3. In the court case *Roberts v. City of Boston* (1850), white lawyer and abolitionist Charles Sumner (1811–1874) argued alongside African American lawyer and plaintiff Robert Morris (1823–1882) to end racial segregation in Boston's schools. Their case was ultimately unsuccessful.

4. Woodson's publication coincides with the rise of New Deal–era legislation under the presidency of Franklin Roosevelt. The reform efforts set a new precedent for federal assistance during the social and economic recovery from the Depression.

CHAPTER XIII.
UNDERSTAND THE NEGRO

1. Fredrika Bremer (1801–1865), Swedish novelist who traveled extensively in the United States, inspiring her book *The Homes of the New World* (1853).

CHAPTER XIV.

THE NEW PROGRAM

1. Richard Allen (1760–1831), minister and educator, founded the African Methodist Episcopal Church in 1794; Henry Evans (1760–1810), preacher, laid the foundation for the first Methodist church in Fayetteville, North Carolina, that served both white and black congregants; while enslaved, George Bentley served as the pastor of a white church in Giles County, Tennessee.

2. William Bagley (1874–1946), Charles Hubbard Judd (1873–1946), and Edward Thorndike (1874–1949) were considered leading educational theorists of the time.

3. José Rizal (1861–1896), Filipino nationalist and writer who was an outspoken critic of Spanish colonial rule in the Philippines.

CHAPTER XV.

VOCATIONAL GUIDANCE

1. Jan Ernst Matzeliger (1852–1889), an inventor born in Dutch Guiana, is credited with inventing the "Lasting Machine," a device designed to improve the technique of connecting the upper flaps to the soles of a shoe.

CHAPTER XVIII.

THE STUDY OF THE NEGRO

1. A region of Africa encompassing what is now Ethiopia and Eritrea.

2. In 1915, Woodson founded the Association for the Study of Negro Life and History, now called the Association for the Study of African American Life and History (ASALH). The association continues as a research and publication outlet for information on black life, history, and culture.